Computerized Accounting Using *Microsoft Dynamics*™ *GP 10.0*

Fourth Edition
2008

REFERENCE

By

Alvin A. Arens
D. Dewey Ward

Professors of Accounting, Emeriti
Michigan State University

TABLE OF CONTENTS

continued on next page

TABLE OF CONTENTS *CONTINUED*

Introduction

Overview

The *Microsoft Dynamics GP* software is intended primarily for a wide variety of medium-size businesses, and is therefore designed to accommodate many different circumstances. As a result, the software has dozens of windows and hundreds of boxes in which to enter or accept information.

To help students learn to use *Microsoft Dynamics GP*, the Reference book is a critical guide to correctly process transactions and do other activities. Based on experience with many students learning to use the software, those who follow the Reference book for each transaction or other activity perform far better than those who do not.

The Reference book contains twenty-two sections, one for each transaction or other activity studied in the *Computerized Accounting Using Microsoft Dynamics GP 10.0* project. See the table of contents for a list of the transactions and activities covered in this book. At the end of the Reference book, in Appendix A, there are materials to assist you in correcting errors if you make them.

Contents of Reference Book

There are five parts to the Reference book. The first three are the most important.

(1) **Transaction or Other Activity Overview.** The brief overview describes what happens in *Microsoft Dynamics GP* for the transaction or other activity being processed. The overview for each section is boxed and located above the Quick Reference Table.

(2) **Quick Reference Table.** The Quick Reference Table is intended as a guide to make certain that you open the correct window(s) and enter or accept the correct information in each box.

(3) **Window(s) on the Page Facing the Quick Reference Table.** The window or windows on the facing page is the window or windows you will be using for the section. Included on the window(s) are circled letters that match the steps on the Quick Reference Table. The letters will not appear on your screen.

(4) Detailed Instructions. Immediately after the Quick Reference Table and related window or windows are detailed instructions for each step in the Quick Reference Table. The purpose of the detail pages is to provide additional guidance for the steps in the Quick Reference Table. The letters on these pages correspond to the circled letters on the Quick Reference Table and the related window or windows.

(5) Error Correction (Appendix A). If you make errors in *Microsoft Dynamics GP* after you post or save transactions, it is often difficult to correct them. In the event that you make errors, Appendix A is intended to help you correct them.

Suggested Way to Use the Reference Book

The following are suggestions to help you effectively use the Reference book:

- Determine the type of transaction you are to record or other activity you are to do. Significant guidance is provided in each chapter of the Instructions and Assignments book to help you.

- Determine the applicable Reference book page numbers. You should do this through the instructions in the chapter or the Reference Summary Card included in the materials.

- Open the Reference book to the first two pages for the transaction or other activity that you will be processing. Follow the step-by-step instructions in the Quick Reference Table and related window or windows.

As you become proficient with *Microsoft Dynamics GP*, at a minimum, you should review all steps in the Quick Reference Table before you post a transaction. It will almost certainly help minimize errors.

This page is intentionally blank.

REVENUE CYCLE ACTIVITIES

Revenue Cycle Activities:

Make A Credit Sale

Overview

The Invoice Entry window is used to process and record a credit sale invoice. After the Invoice Entry window is posted, the accounts receivable subsidiary records and the perpetual inventory records are updated for the effects of the transaction. Later, when the transaction is posted to the general ledger, accounts receivable and cost of goods sold are debited and sales revenue, inventory, and sales taxes payable are credited.

Quick Reference Table

Step	Box or Other Location	Procedure
A	Navigation Pane buttons	Click *Sales* → *Invoice Entry (T)*.
B	Document Type	Accept Invoice as the document type.
C	Document No.	Accept the default invoice number or type the correct invoice number.
D	Date	Review the default invoice date and change if necessary.
E	Customer ID	Select the Customer ID.
F	Customer PO Number	Type the customer's purchase order number, if applicable.
G	Show button	Click the Show button.
H	Item Number	Select the inventory item sold.
I	Quantity	Accept the default quantity sold or type the correct quantity.
J	Markdown box and expansion button	Enter price markdown information, if applicable.
K	Next blank Item Number box	Move the cursor to the next blank Item Number box.
L	Various	Repeat steps H through K for each type of inventory item sold.
M	Distributions button	Click the Distributions button.
N	Invoice Distribution Entry window (not shown)	Verify the general ledger account distributions.
O	Invoice Entry window	Review the Invoice Entry window for completeness and accuracy.
P	Post button	Post the invoice.

Make A Credit Sale
Dynamics Window

Invoice Entry Window
Sales → Invoice Entry (T) **A**

Invoice Entry — □ ☒

File   Edit   Tools   Options **P**   sa Jackson Supply Company 2/1/2010

💾 **Save** | ✕ <u>D</u>elete | 📧 <u>P</u>ost | 🖨 Print |

Document Type	Invoice **B** ▾	Date 2/1/2010 **D** ▦ →
Document No.	**C** 🔍📄	<u>Default Site</u> MAIN 🔍📄
☐ Hold		Batch ID 🔍📄 →
<u>Customer ID</u>	**E** 🔍📄 →	Customer PO Number **F**
Name		Currency ID 🔍📄

<u>Item Number</u> 🔍📄 →	U of M 🔍	Quantity	<u>Unit Price</u>	☆
Description	Unit Cost	Markdown **J** →	Extended Price	☆
H		**I** 0.00	$0.00	∧
	$0.00	**J** $0.00	$0.00	
K				
L				
				∨

Amount Received	$0.00 →	Subtotal	$0.00	
Terms Discount Taken	$0.00 →	Trade Discount	$0.00	
On Account	$0.00	Freight	$0.00	→
<u>Comment ID</u>	🔍📄 →	Miscellaneous	$0.00	→
		Tax	$0.00	→
M Distributions	Commissions	Total	$0.00	

|◀ ◀ ▶ ▶| by Document No. ▾   📄 ⑦

G (right side)

Make A Credit Sale
Detailed Instructions

A. Click *Sales* → *Invoice Entry (T)*

> *Click Sales → Invoice Entry (T) to access the Invoice Entry window.*

B. Accept Invoice as the Document Type

The Invoice Entry window can be used to enter both sales invoices and sales returns. The default for the box is Invoice.

> *Accept Invoice as the document type.*

C. Accept the Default Invoice Number or Type the Correct Invoice Number

Microsoft Dynamics GP automatically assigns the next sequential invoice number in the Document No. box.

> *Accept the default invoice number or type the correct invoice number.*

D. Review the Default Invoice Date and Change if Necessary

> *If the invoice date is different than the date shown, type the correct date.*

E. Select the Customer ID

> *Use the adjacent lookup button to select the customer ID.*

F. Type the Customer's Purchase Order Number, if Applicable

> *If the customer submits a purchase order, type the purchase order number. If there is no purchase order, skip the box.*

G. Click the Show Button

A Show button appears in the Invoice Entry window to the right of the description field "Extended Price". The Show button reveals the boxes related to the second line of description fields for the scrolling window below (Description, Unit Cost, Markdown, and Extended Price). You need to access these boxes to enter the sale of inventory items.

➤ *Click the Show button to reveal all boxes in the scrolling window below.*

H. Select the Inventory Item Sold

➤ *Use the Item Number lookup button to select the inventory item sold.*

I. Accept the Default Quantity Sold or Type the Correct Quantity

➤ *Either accept the default quantity sold of 1 or type the correct quantity.*

J. Enter Price Markdown Information, if Applicable

The Markdown box is used to enter a price reduction for an inventory item. If there is a price reduction for the item, complete the following five steps:

➤ (1) *Click the Markdown box for the item being sold at a reduced price.*
➤ (2) *Click the Markdown expansion button to access the Invoice Markdown Entry window.*
➤ (3) *In the Invoice Markdown Entry window, click either the Percentage button or the Amount button, depending on the type of markdown. The default button is the Percentage button.*
➤ (4) *Type the price reduction percentage or amount in the box adjacent to the Percentage and Amount buttons.*
➤ (5) *Click the OK button to save the price reduction information.*

K. Move the Cursor to the Next Blank Item Number Box

➤ *Move through the remaining boxes for the item sold until the cursor enters the first blank Item Number box below.*

L. Repeat Steps H through K for Each Type of Inventory Item Sold

➤ Continue entering information for each type of inventory item sold. After you have entered all information for the last item sold, make sure you move the cursor to the next blank Item Number box. This allows Microsoft Dynamics GP to complete all window calculations (including the amount in the Tax box).

M. Click the Distributions Button

Once the last inventory item sold has been entered into the Invoice Entry window, you are ready to review the general ledger account distributions and edit them if necessary.

➤ Click the Distributions button to access the Invoice Distribution Entry window.

N. Verify the General Ledger Account Distributions

Microsoft Dynamics GP automatically distributes amounts from the transaction to general ledger accounts based on information on file for the selected customer and the inventory items sold. These accounts are visible in the Invoice Distribution Entry window.

The cost of goods sold and inventory portions of the entry do not show here, but the correct postings to these accounts are made when the invoice is posted. Because *Microsoft Dynamics GP* is designed to accommodate a multiple-user environment, and because many companies use inventory methods that are dependent upon when a transaction occurs (LIFO, FIFO, etc.), cost of goods sold and inventory calculations are not made until each sale transaction is posted.

➤ Click the Show button to display detailed general ledger account information for each posting account.

➤ If the account distributions are correct, close the window.

➤ To change an account distribution, click anywhere on the five-digit account number to be changed. Either type the new account number or click the Account lookup button to select the correct account number. Once all account distribution changes are made, click the OK button to save the changes and to return to the Invoice Entry window.

O. Review the Invoice Entry Window for Completeness and Accuracy

Before the invoice is posted, most errors can be corrected by clicking the box with the error and making the correction. If you discover that an incorrect item number was entered for inventory sold, *Microsoft Dynamics GP* does not allow you to change the item number without first deleting the line with the incorrect item number on it.

Certain boxes cannot be changed after they are originally completed. Errors in these boxes can only be corrected by deleting the transaction and entering the transaction again.

> *Review the Invoice Entry window for completeness and accuracy. If you find an error while reviewing the window, click the box with the error and make corrections. If you need to change the Item Number box for an inventory item sold, click any box for that item (Item Number, Description, Unit Price, etc.), click the Edit menu, then click the Delete Row option. Reenter all information for the correct item number sold.*

> *If the box with the error cannot be accessed or changed, click the Delete button and click Delete again when asked if you are sure that you want to delete this record. Enter the transaction again by returning to step B.*

P. Post the Invoice

The transaction is posted from the Invoice Entry window using the Post button. Clicking the Post button posts the transaction to the customer and inventory subsidiary records, but does not post the transaction to the general ledger. Posting to the general ledger is discussed on pages 154–157.

> *After you are satisfied with all of the data in the Invoice Entry window, click the Post button to post the invoice.*

> *Close the Invoice Entry window.*

Transaction Review

After clicking the Post button in the Invoice Entry window, you can determine if the transaction has been posted to the subsidiary records by completing the steps that follow. Recall that the invoice has not yet been posted to the general ledger.

> *Click Sales → Transaction by Document (I) to open the Receivables Transaction Inquiry - Document window.*

Posted receivables transactions by document are shown in the scrolling window of the Receivables Transaction Inquiry - Document window. All invoices contain the letters "SLS" in the Type box of the scrolling window.

 Click once on the line containing the invoice just posted. With the selected invoice highlighted, move the mouse pointer over the Document Number description field until the pointer turns into a hand.

 When the hand appears, click once on the Document Number description field to zoom to the Invoice Inquiry window for the selected invoice.

The window that appears is a replica of the Invoice Entry window for the selected invoice. It is not possible to change information through the Invoice Inquiry window. You can review the account distributions for the selected invoice by clicking the Distributions button. Observe that the inventory and cost of goods sold amounts have been automatically posted by *Microsoft Dynamics GP*. By clicking the Show button, you can review details for each inventory item sold.

 Close the Invoice Inquiry window and the Receivables Transaction Inquiry - Document window.

Error Correction After Posting a Transaction

If you discover an error after posting a credit sale, refer to Appendix A.

This page is intentionally blank.

Make A Cash Sale

Overview

The Invoice Entry and the Invoice Payment Entry windows are used to process and record a cash sale and the corresponding customer payment. When the windows are posted, the perpetual inventory records are updated. Later, when the transaction is posted to the general ledger, cash and cost of goods sold are debited and sales revenue, inventory, and sales taxes payable are credited.

Quick Reference Table

Step	Box or Other Location	Procedure
A	Navigation Pane buttons	Click *Sales* → *Invoice Entry (T)*.
B	Document Type	Accept Invoice as the document type
C	Document No.	Accept the default invoice number or type the correct number.
D	Date	Review the default invoice date and change if necessary.
E	Customer ID	Select the Customer ID that applies to cash customers.
F	Name	Type the customer's name.
G	Customer PO Number	Type the customer's purchase order number, if applicable.
H	Show button	Click the Show button.
I	Item Number	Select the inventory item sold.
J	Quantity	Accept the default quantity sold or type the correct quantity.
K	Markdown box and expansion button	Enter price markdown information, if applicable.
L	Next blank Item No. box	Move the cursor to the next blank Item Number box.
M	Various	Repeat steps I through L for each type of inventory item sold.
N	Amount Received	Type the amount received from the customer.*
O**	Payment Type	Review the payment type and change if necessary.
P**	Check Number	For checks only, type the customer's check number.
Q**	Date	Review the customer payment date and change if necessary.
R**	Insert button	Click the Insert button.
S**	OK button	Click the OK button.
T	Distributions button (Invoice Entry window)	Click the Distributions button.
U	Invoice Distribution Entry window (not shown)	Verify the general ledger account distributions.
V	Invoice Entry window	Review the Invoice Entry window for completeness and accuracy.
W	Post button	Post the cash sale.

Note: You must also record the bank deposit. See pages 48–51.
   *   This opens the Invoice Payment Entry window.
   **   Steps O-S are in the Invoice Payment Entry window.

Make A Cash Sale
Dynamics Windows

Invoice Entry Window
Sales → Invoice Entry (T) (A)

(V)

Invoice Entry

File   Edit   Tools   Options   (W)   sa Jackson Supply Company 2/1/2010

💾 Save   ✖ Delete   ⊞ Post   🖨 Print

Document Type	Invoice (B) (C)	Date 2/1/2010 (D)
Document No.		Default Site MAIN
☐ Hold		Batch ID
Customer ID	(E) (F)	Customer PO Number (G)
Name		Currency ID

Item Number	U of M	Quantity (K)	Unit Price
Description	Unit Cost	Markdown (J)	Extended Price
(I)		0.00	$0.00
(L)	$0.00	(K) $0.00	$0.00
(M)			

Amount Received	$0.00 (N)	Subtotal	$0.00
Terms Discount Taken	$0.00	Trade Discount	$0.00
On Account	$0.00	Freight	$0.00
Comment ID		Miscellaneous	$0.00
		Tax	$0.00
(T) Distributions Commissions		Total	$0.00

◄◄ ◄ ► ►◄   by Document No.

(H)

Invoice Payment Entry Window

Invoice Payment Entry

File   Edit   Tools   Help   sa Jackson Supply Company 2/1/2010

Amount Received	$552.50	COD Amount	$0.00

Payment Type:	Check (O)	Card Name	
Checkbook ID	OHIO	Card Number	
Check Number	1002 (P)	Expiration Date	0/0/0000
Date	2/1/2010 (Q)	Authorization Code	
Cash Receipt Number	PYMNT000000000036		
Currency ID			
Payment Amount	$552.50		

Payment Type	Date	Currency ID	Payment Amount
Checkbook/Card Name	Check/Card Number		Document

(R) Insert >>

Remove

Total Payments Distributed: $0.00

(S) OK   Clear

Make A Cash Sale
Detailed Instructions

Entering a cash sale invoice is similar to entering a credit sale invoice because both transaction types use the Invoice Entry window. For cash sale invoices, however, an additional window is used to enter the payment received from the customer.

Because of the similarity of the two transaction types, the following outline focuses on how processing a cash sale invoice differs from processing a credit sale invoice. See the Make A Credit Sale section on pages 6-12 for additional detailed instructions.

A. Click *Sales → Invoice Entry (T)*

➤ *Click Sales → Invoice Entry (T) to access the Invoice Entry window.*

B. Accept Invoice as the Document Type

➤ *Accept Invoice as the document type.*

C. Accept the Default Invoice Number or Type the Correct Number

Microsoft Dynamics GP automatically assigns the next sequential invoice number in the Document No. Box. If cash sales invoices use a different numbering system, type the correct cash sale invoice number.

➤ *Accept the default invoice number or type the correct number.*

D. Review the Default Invoice Date and Change if Necessary

➤ *If the invoice date is different than the date shown, type the correct date.*

E. Select the Customer ID that Applies to Cash Customers

The companies used in this project use one customer ID for all cash customers. This allows the use of default data for all cash customers and reduces the amount of data entry required for each cash sale.

➤ *Use the Customer ID lookup button to select the customer ID that applies to cash customers.*

F. Type the Customer's Name

For cash customers, the Name box is blank. You must type the name of the customer.

➤ *Type the customer's name.*

G. Type the Customer's Purchase Order Number, if Applicable

➤ *If the customer submits a purchase order, type the purchase order number. If there is no purchase order, skip the box.*

H. Click the Show Button

The Show button functions the same for a cash sale as for a credit sale.

➤ *Click the Show button to show the boxes in the scrolling window below.*

I. Select the Inventory Item Sold

➤ *Use the Item Number lookup button to select the inventory item sold.*

J. Accept the Default Quantity Sold or Type the Correct Quantity

➤ *Either accept the default quantity sold of 1 or type the correct quantity.*

K. Enter Price Markdown Information, if Applicable

➤ *Enter price markdown information, if applicable.*

L. Move the Cursor to the Next Blank Item Number Box

➤ *Move through the remaining boxes for the item sold until the cursor enters the first blank Item Number box below.*

M. Repeat Steps I through L for Each Type of Inventory Item Sold

➤ *Continue entering information for each type of inventory item sold. After you have entered all information for the last item sold, make sure that you move the cursor to the next blank Item Number box.* This allows the software to complete all window calculations (including the amount in the Tax box).

N. Type the Amount Received from the Customer

The Amount Received box is used to enter the customer's payment for the cash sale. Because it is a cash sale, the amount received must match the total invoice amount.

Review the total invoice amount in the bottom right corner of the window. The amount received must equal the invoice total. Type the amount received. When you press [Return], the Invoice Payment Entry window opens automatically (see bottom of page 15 for an illustration).

At this point you will have two windows open, the Invoice Payment Entry window and the Invoice Entry window. To move back and forth between them, click on the Windows option on the Menu Bar at the top of the screen. This will list all the windows that are open and you simply click on the one you want on top. To continue with the recording of a cash sale, keep the Invoice Payment Entry window on top.

O. Review the Payment Type and Change if Necessary

The Payment Type box in the Invoice Payment Entry window is used to enter the form of payment received from the customer. Cash customers either pay in cash, by check, or with a credit/bank card. For this project, only payments made in cash or by check are described.

Use the Payment Type drop-down list to select the customer's method of payment.

P. For Checks Only, Type the Customer's Check Number

If the customer pays by check, type the customer's check number in the Check Number box. If you cannot type a check number, you selected the wrong payment type in step O.

Q. Review the Customer Payment Date and Change if Necessary

The Date box contains the same date entered in the Invoice Entry window. If the customer payment date is different, type the payment date.

Review the contents of the Date box and, if necessary, change the date to the date of the customer's payment.

R. Click the Insert Button

 Review the contents of the Invoice Payment Entry window for completeness and accuracy. When you are satisfied with all of the information, click the Insert button to insert the amount of the payment into the lower half of the window, which shows the distribution of the payment.

After inserting, you can click on the Show button in the Payment Distribution box to see the details of the payment. Do not be concerned that after clicking Insert, some of the information at the top changes: the Cash Receipt Number increments by one and the Payment Type reverts to the default value, Cash. Only the information in the Payment Distribution box will be posted for this transaction.

S. Click the OK Button

 Click the OK button to save the payment information and to return to the Invoice Entry window.

T. Click the Distributions Button

 Click the Distributions button to open the Invoice Distribution Entry window.

U. Verify the General Ledger Account Distributions

 Click the Show button to display detailed general ledger account information for each posting account.

 Review general ledger account distributions and, if necessary, change them.

 Click the OK button to return to the Invoice Entry window.

V. Review the Invoice Entry Window for Completeness and Accuracy

 Review the Invoice Entry window for completeness and accuracy.

 If there are errors, correct them.

W. Post the Cash Sale

 After you are satisfied with all of the data in the Invoice Entry window, click the Post button to post the cash sale invoice.

Transaction Review

After clicking the Post button in the Invoice Entry window, you can determine if the transaction has been posted to the subsidiary records by completing the steps that follow. Recall that the transaction has not yet been posted to the general ledger.

➤ *Click Sales → Transaction by Document (I) to open the Receivables Transaction Inquiry–Document window.*

➤ *Click once on the line containing the cash sale invoice just posted, (not the cash receipt portion of the transaction). Both the invoice and the cash receipt are included in the scrolling window. Sales invoices are identified by the letters "SLS" in the Type box. With the selected invoice highlighted, move the mouse pointer over the Document Number description field until the pointer turns into a hand.*

➤ *When the hand appears, click the Document Number description field to zoom to the Invoice Inquiry window for the selected invoice.*

The window that appears is a replica of the Invoice Entry window for the selected invoice. It is not possible to change information through the Invoice Inquiry window. You can review the account distributions for the selected invoice by clicking the Distributions button. By clicking the Show button, you can review details of for each inventory item sold.

➤ *Close the Invoice Inquiry window to return to the Receivables Transaction Inquiry–Document window.*

Because a cash invoice also involves a customer payment, you can also zoom to the payment portion of the cash sale transaction.

➤ *Click once on the line containing the payment portion of the cash sale invoice just posted. Payments are identified by the letters "PMT" in the Type box of the scrolling window. With the selected payment highlighted, move the mouse pointer over the Document Number description field until the pointer turns into a hand.*

➤ *When the hand glass appears, click the Document Number description field to zoom to the Cash Receipts Inquiry Zoom window for the posted cash sale transaction.*

➤ *Close the Cash Receipts Inquiry Zoom and Receivables Transaction Inquiry–Document windows.*

Error Correction After Posting the Transaction

If you discover an error after posting a cash sale, refer to Appendix A.

Receive Goods on a Sales Return

Overview

The Invoice Entry window is used to process and record a sales return. After the Invoice Entry window is posted, the accounts receivable subsidiary records and the perpetual inventory records are updated. Later, when the transaction is posted to the general ledger, sales returns and allowances, inventory, and sales taxes payable are debited and accounts receivable and cost of goods sold are credited.

The second window used for sales returns is the Apply Sales Document window, which is used to update the accounts receivable subsidiary record by applying the sales return to a specific invoice or invoices. Because applying a sales return is not a transaction, it does not affect the total amounts in the accounts receivable subsidiary records or in the general ledger.

Quick Reference Table

Step	Box or Other Location	Procedure
A	Navigation Pane buttons	Click Sales ➔ Invoice Entry (T).
B	Document Type	Select Return as the document type.
C	Document No.	Accept the default sales return document number or type the correct number.
D	Date	Review the default sales return date and change if necessary.
E	Customer ID	Select the Customer ID.
F	Customer PO Number	Type the customer's sales return request number, if applicable.
G	Show button	Click the Show button.
H	Item Number	Select the inventory item returned.
I	Quantity	Type the quantity returned, complete the Invoice Returned Quantities Entry window, and click the OK button.
J	Markdown box and expansion button	Enter price markdown information, if applicable.
K	Next blank Item Number box	Move the cursor to the next blank Item Number box.
L	Various	Repeat steps H through K for each type of inventory item returned.
M	Distributions button	Click the Distributions button.
N	Invoice Distr. Entry window (not shown)	Verify the general ledger account distributions.
O	Invoice Entry window	Review the Invoice Entry window for completeness and accuracy.
P	Post button	Post the sales return.
Q	Close button	Close the Invoice Entry window.
R	Navigation Pane buttons	Click Sales ➔ Apply Sales Documents (T).
S	Customer ID	Select the customer ID.
T	Type	Select Returns as the type of transaction being applied.
U	Document No.	Select the sales return document being applied.
V	Apply Date / Apply Posting Date	Review the apply date and the apply posting date and change if necessary.
W	Check box(es)	Select the invoice(s) to which the sales return is being applied.
X	Apply Sales Documents Window	Review the Apply Sales Document window for completeness and accuracy.
Y	OK button	Click the OK button to save the applied information.

Receive Goods on a Sales Return
Dynamics Windows

Invoice Entry Window
Sales → Invoice Entry (T) **A**

O **Invoice Entry** **Q**

File Edit Tools Options **P**   sa Jackson Supply Company 2/1/2010

💾 Save   ✕ Delete   📧 Post   🖨 Print

Document Type	Return **B** **C** 🔍📄
Document No.	1503
☐ Hold	

Date	2/1/2010 **D**
Default Site	MAIN 🔍📄
Batch ID	🔍📄→

Customer ID **E** 🔍📄→   Customer PO Number **F**
Name   Currency ID

Item Number 🔍📄→	U of M 🔍	Quantity	Unit Price	≫
Description	Unit Cost	Markdown **J** →	Extended Price	≫
H		**I** 0.00	$0.00	
	$0.00	**J** $0.00	$0.00	
K				
L {				

Amount Received	$0.00 →	
Discount Returned	$0.00	
On Account	$0.00	
Comment ID	🔍📄→	

Subtotal	$0.00
Trade Discount	$0.00
Freight	$0.00 →
Miscellaneous	$0.00 →
Tax	$0.00 →
Total	$0.00

M Distributions   Commissions

⏮ ◀ ▶ ⏭ by Document No.   **G**

Apply Sales Documents Window
Sales → Apply Sales Documents (T) **R**

X **Apply Sales Documents**

File **Y** Edit Tools Help   sa Jackson Supply Company 2/1/2010

✓ OK   🔍 Find   Unapply   Auto Apply

Customer ID MCCA0001 **S** **T** 🔍   Name McCarthy's Bed & Breakfast
Type: Returns   Apply From Currency ID

Document No. ◀ 1503 **U** ▶ 🔍   Original Amount $517.13
Apply Date   2/1/2010 **V**   Unapplied Amount $517.13
Apply Posting Date **V** 2/1/2010

Apply to Document	Due Date	Amount Remaining	Apply Amount	≫
Type / Original Document Amt	Discount Date / Terms Available	Terms Taken	Writeoffs	
Apply To Currency ID / Exchange Rate	Calculation Method	Realized Gain/Loss		
W ☐ 5126001	2/19/2009	$3,131.36	$0.00	

⏮ ◀ ▶ ⏭ by Customer ID

Receive Goods on a Sales Return
Detailed Instructions

Entering a sales return is similar to entering a credit sale because both transaction types use the Invoice Entry window. Because of their similarity, the following outline emphasizes the differences in processing a sales return. See the Make A Credit Sale section on pages 6-12 for additional detailed instructions.

A. Click *Sales → Invoice Entry (T)*

➡ *Click Sales → Invoice Entry (T) to access the Invoice Entry window.*

B. Select Return as the Document Type

➡ *Use the Document Type drop-down list to select Return as the type of document.*

C. Accept the Default Sales Return Document Number or Type the Correct Number

Microsoft Dynamics GP automatically assigns the next sequential sales return document number (such as a credit memo number) in the Document No. box.

➡ *Accept the default sales return document number or type the correct number.*

D. Review the Default Sales Return Date and Change if Necessary

➡ *If the date of the sales return transaction is different than the date shown, type the correct date.*

E. Select the Customer ID

➡ *Use the adjacent lookup button to select the customer ID.*

F. Type the Customer's Sales Return Request Number, if Applicable

➡ *If the customer submits a document with the sales return, such as a sales return request, type the customer's document number in the Customer PO box. If there is no such document, skip the box.*

G. Click the Show Button

➤ *Click the Show button to reveal all boxes in the scrolling window below.*

H. Select the Inventory Item Returned

➤ *Use the Item Number lookup button to select the inventory item returned.*

I. Type the Quantity Returned, Complete the Invoice Returned Quantities Entry Window, and Click the OK Button

➤ *Type the quantity returned.*

After the quantity returned is typed, the Invoice Returned Quantities Entry window appears. The window is used to select a quantity type for the items returned. Five quantity types exist, as shown in the Return Quantity Type section of the window:

- **On Hand**   Returned items that are available for resale.
- **Returned**   Returned items that are not yet available for resale.
- **In Use**   Returned items that are being used by the company. An example would be an item used for sales demonstrations.
- **In Service**   Returned items that are being repaired.
- **Damaged**   Returned items that are damaged.

➤ *Type the quantity returned in the appropriate Return Quantity Type boxes. For example, if 5 items are returned, 4 that can be sold to another customer and 1 that is damaged, type [4] in the On Hand box and [1] in the Damaged box.*

➤ *Click the OK button to return to the Invoice Entry window.*

J. Enter Price Markdown Information, if Applicable

If the inventory was originally sold at a reduced price, the sales return must be processed using the same price reduction.

➤ *Enter the price markdown information, if applicable.*

K. Move the Cursor to the Next Blank Item Number Box

➤ *Move through the remaining boxes for the item returned until the cursor enters the first blank Item Number box below.*

L. Repeat Steps H through K for Each Type of Inventory Item Returned

➤ *Continue entering information for each type of inventory item returned. After you have entered all information for the last item returned, make sure that you move the cursor to the next blank Item Number box.* This allows the software to complete all window calculations (including the amount in the Tax box).

M. Click the Distributions Button

➤ *Click the Distributions button to access the Invoice Distribution Entry window.*

N. Verify the General Ledger Account Distributions

➤ *Click the Show button to display detailed general ledger account information for each posting account.*

➤ *If the account distributions are correct, click OK to close the window.*

➤ *If the account distributions are not correct, correct the distributions and click the OK button to save the changes and to return to the Invoice Entry window.*

O. Review the Invoice Entry Window for Completeness and Accuracy

➤ *Review the Invoice Entry window for completeness and accuracy.*

➤ *If there are errors, correct them.*

P. Post the Sales Return

➤ *After you are satisfied with all of the data in the Invoice Entry window, click the Post button to post the sales return.*

Q. Close the Invoice Entry Window

➤ *Close the Invoice Entry window.*

R. Click *Sales → Apply Sales Documents (T)*

➤ *Click Sales → Apply Sales Documents (T) to access the Apply Sales Documents window.*

S. Select the Customer ID

→ *Use the adjacent lookup button to select the customer ID.*

T. Select Returns as the Type of Transaction being Applied

The Apply Sales Documents window is used to apply credit memos, returns, and payments to outstanding invoices.

→ *Use the adjacent drop-down list to select Returns as the type of transaction being applied.*

U. Select the Sales Return Document being Applied

→ *Use the adjacent lookup button to select the sales return document being applied.*

After selecting the sales return document, the scrolling window in the bottom half of the Apply Sales Documents window fills with all current year invoices for the selected customer.

V. Review the Apply Date and the Apply Posting Date and Change if Necessary

→ *If the date of the sales return transaction is different than the dates shown, type the correct date in both boxes.*

W. Select the Invoice(s) to which the Sales Return is being Applied

A check box appears on the left side of each invoice in the scrolling window. These check boxes are used to select the invoice(s) to which the sales return will be applied.

→ *Locate the first invoice to which the sales return will be applied. Click the check box next to that invoice. Repeat this step with additional invoices until the sales return is fully applied.*

When the sales return is fully applied, the amount in the Unapplied Amount box will be zero.

X. Review the Apply Sales Documents Window for Completeness and Accuracy

- *Review the Apply Sales Documents window for completeness and accuracy.*
- *If there are errors, correct them.*

Y. Click the OK Button to Save the Applied Information

- *Click the OK button to save the information.*

Transaction Review

Transaction review for the Invoice Entry window was discussed in the Make A Credit Sale section on pages 11 and 12. Refer to these pages for detailed instructions. The only difference between reviewing a sales invoice and reviewing a sales return is that sales returns contain the letters "RTN" in the Type box of the scrolling window, instead of "SLS."

Error Correction After Posting and Applying the Transaction

If you discover an error after posting or applying a sales return transaction, refer to Appendix A.

This page is intentionally blank.

Collect an Outstanding Account Receivable

Overview

The Cash Receipts Entry and Apply Sales Documents windows are used to process and record a collection of an account receivable. After the windows are posted, the transaction updates the accounts receivable subsidiary records. Later, when the transaction is posted to the general ledger, cash and sales discounts are debited, and accounts receivable is credited.

Quick Reference Table

Step	Box or Other Location	Procedure
A	Navigation Pane buttons	Click *Sales* ➔ *Cash Receipts (T)*.
B	Date	Review the default cash receipt date and change if necessary.
C	Customer ID	Select the Customer ID.
D	Check or Cash radio button	Select the type of payment received: check or cash.
E	Amount	Type the amount of the cash receipt.
F	Check/Card Number	For checks only, type the check number.
G	Apply button	Click the Apply button.
H	Show button (Steps H-J are in the Apply Sales Documents window)	Click the Show button.
I	Check box(es)	Select the invoice(s) to which the cash receipt is being applied.
J	OK button	Click the OK button.
K	Distribution button	Click the Distribution button.
L	Cash Receipts Distribution Entry window (not shown)	Verify the general ledger account distributions.
M	Cash Receipts Entry window	Review the Cash Receipts Entry window for completeness and accuracy.
N	Post button	Post the cash receipt.

Note: You must also record the bank deposit. See pages 48-51.

Collect an Outstanding Account Receivable
Dynamics Windows

Cash Receipts Entry Window
Sales → Cash Receipts (T) (A)

(M)

Cash Receipts Entry

File   Edit   Tools   Help   (N)   sa Jackson Supply Company 2/1/2010

💾 **Save** | 🔲 Auto Apply | 🔲 Post | ✖ Delete

Receipt	PYMNT000000000036|

Batch ID   (B)
Date   2/1/2010

Customer ID   (C)
Name
Currency ID

Locate Customer By:
Document

(D)   (D)

⦿ Check   ◯ Cash   ◯ Credit Card

(E)

Amount
Checkbook ID   OHIO
Credit Card ID
Check/Card Number   (F)
Comment

(G) Apply

(K) Distribution

|◀ ◀ ▶ ▶| by Receipt   Status   Unsaved

Apply Sales Documents Window

Apply Sales Documents

File (J) lit   Tools   Help   sa Jackson Supply Company 2/1/2010

✓ OK | 🔍 Find | 🔲 Unapply | 🔲 Auto Apply

Customer ID	MCCA0001	Name	McCarthy's Bed & Breakfast
Type:	Payments	Apply From Currency ID	

Document No.   ◀ PYMNT000000000036 ▶   Original Amount $1,000.00
Apply Date   2/1/2010   Unapplied Amount $1,000.00
Apply Posting Date   2/1/2010

Apply to Document	Due Date	Amount Remaining	Apply Amount	⌃
Type	Original Document Amt	Discount Date	Terms Available	Terms Taken	Writeoffs	⌄
Apply To Currency ID	Exchange Rate	Calculation Method	Realized Gain/Loss	

(I) ☐ 5126001   2/19/2009 $3,131.36 $0.00
SLS $3,286.50 1/30/2009 $62.60 $0.00 $0.00
          0.0000000 $0.00

(H)

|◀ ◀ ▶ ▶| by Customer ID

Collect an Outstanding Account Receivable
Detailed Instructions

A. Click *Sales* → *Cash Receipts (T)*

> ➤ *Click Sales → Cash Receipts (T) to access the Cash Receipts Entry window.*

B. Review the Default Cash Receipt Date and Change if Necessary

> ➤ *If the date of the cash receipt is different than the date shown, type the correct date.*

C. Select the Customer ID

> ➤ *Use the adjacent lookup button to select the customer ID.*

D. Select the Type of Payment Received: Check or Cash

> ➤ *The default type of payment received is Check. Press [Return] to accept Check or click the Cash radio button.* Credit card receipts are not covered in this project.

E. Type the Amount of the Cash Receipt

> ➤ *Type the amount of the cash receipt.*

F. For Checks Only, Type the Check Number

> ➤ *For checks received, type the check number.*
> ➤ *For cash received, skip the Check/Card Number box.*

G. Click the Apply Button

Cash receipts must be applied to outstanding invoices. The process is done through the Apply Sales Documents window, which is accessed from the Cash Receipts Entry window by clicking the Apply button. The Apply Sales Documents window was discussed in the Receive Goods on a Sales Return section on pages 22-28. The same window is used to apply cash receipts to outstanding invoices.

➨ *Click the Apply button to access the Apply Sales Documents window.*

H. Click the Show Button

➨ *Click the Show button to reveal all boxes in the scrolling window below.*

I. Select the Invoice(s) to Which the Cash Receipt is being Applied

➨ *Locate the first invoice to which the cash receipt is being applied. Click the check box next to that invoice. Repeat this step with additional invoices until the cash receipt is fully applied.*

J. Click the OK Button

➨ *When the cash receipt has been fully applied, click the OK button to save the information and to return to the Cash Receipts Entry window.*

K. Click the Distribution Button

➨ *Click the Distribution button to view the Cash Receipts Distribution Entry window.*

L. Verify the General Ledger Account Distributions

➨ *Click the Show button to display detailed general ledger account information for each posting account.*

➨ *Verify the account distributions. Make changes if necessary and click the OK button when they are correct.*

M. Review the Cash Receipts Entry Window for Completeness and Accuracy

Review the Cash Receipts Entry window for completeness and accuracy. If you find an error while reviewing the window, click on the box with the error and make corrections.

If the box with the error cannot be accessed or changed, click the Delete button and click Delete again when asked if you are sure that you want to delete. Enter the transaction again by returning to step B.

N. Post the Cash Receipt

After you are satisfied with all of the data in the Cash Receipts Entry window, click the Post button to post the account receivable collection.

Transaction Review

Transaction review for accounts receivable collection is similar to transaction review for sales and sales returns [click *Sales → Transaction by Document (I)*]. The only difference is that in the Receivables Transaction Inquiry - Document window, all customer collections contain the letters "PMT" in the Type box of the scrolling window.

Error Correction After Posting the Transaction

If you discover an error after posting an account receivable collection transaction, refer to Appendix A.

This page is intentionally blank.

Write-off an Uncollectible Account Receivable

Overview

The Receivables Transaction Entry window is used to process and record a write-off of an account receivable. After the write-off is processed, the transaction updates the accounts receivable subsidiary records. Later, when the transaction is posted to the general ledger, an allowance account or bad debt expense is debited (depending upon the company's accounting policy) and accounts receivable is credited.

Quick Reference Table

Step	Box or Other Location	Procedure
A	Navigation Pane buttons	Click *Sales → Transaction Entry (T)*.
B	Document Type	Select Credit Memos as the document type.
C	Description	Type a description of the transaction.
D	Document Date	Review the default write-off date and change if necessary.
E	Customer ID	Select the Customer ID.
F	Credit Amount	Type the amount of the write-off.
G	Apply button	Click the Apply button.
H	Apply Sales Documents window (not shown)	Apply the write-off to outstanding invoice(s).
I	Distribution button	Click the Distribution button.
J	Sales Transaction Distribution Entry window (not shown)	Verify the general ledger account distributions.
K	Receivables Transaction Entry window	Review the Receivables Transaction Entry window for completeness and accuracy.
L	Post button	Post the write-off transaction.

Write-off an Uncollectible Account Receivable
Dynamics Window

Receivables Transaction Entry Window
Sales → *Transaction Entry (T)* (A)

(K) **Receivables Transaction Entry**

File　Edit　Tools　Options　(L)　Help　　　　sa Jackson Supply Company 2/1/2010

💾 **Save** ✕ Delete ⊞ Post 🖨 Print

Document Type:	Credit Memos (B)	Batch ID
Number	CR1	Document Date　2/1/2010 (D)
Description	(C)	

Customer ID (E)　　　　Currency ID
Name　　　　　　　　　Payment Terms
Address ID　　　　　　　Shipping Method
Salesperson ID　　　　　Tax Schedule ID
Territory ID　　　　　　P.O. Number

Cost	$0.00	Cash	$0.00
Credit Amount (F)	$0.00	Check	$0.00
Trade Discount	$0.00	Credit Card	$0.00
Freight	$0.00	Discount Returned	
Miscellaneous	$0.00	On Account	$0.00
Tax	$0.00		
Total	$0.00		

(G) Apply　(I) Distribution　Commissions

◄◄ ◄ ► ►◄　by Document　　Status　Unsaved

Write-off an Uncollectible Account Receivable
Detailed Instructions

A. Click *Sales* → *Transaction Entry (T)*

➤ *Click Sales → Transaction Entry (T) to access the Receivables Transaction Entry window.*

B. Select Credit Memos as the Document Type

Write-offs of uncollectible accounts receivable are processed as credit memos in *Microsoft Dynamics GP.*

➤ *Select Credit Memos from the Document Type drop-down list.*

C. Type a Description of the Transaction

An example of an appropriate description for a write-off would be: "Write-off uncollectible amount".

➤ *Type a description of the write-off transaction.*

D. Review the Default Write-off Date and Change if Necessary

➤ *If the date of the write-off transaction is different than the date shown, type the correct date in the Document Date box.*

E. Select the Customer ID

➤ *Use the adjacent lookup button to select the customer ID.*

F. Type the Amount of the Write-off

➤ *Type the amount of the write-off in the Credit Amount box.*

G. Click the Apply Button

Click the Apply button to access the Apply Sales Documents window.

The Apply Sales Documents window is the same window that is used for applying sales returns and cash receipts to outstanding invoices. See pages 22-28 for more information about the Apply Sales Documents window.

H. Apply the Write-off to Outstanding Invoice(s)

Click the check box next to the invoice(s) being written off. When the write-off is fully applied, the amount in the Unapplied Amount box will be zero. Click the OK button to save the application information and to return to the Receivables Transaction Entry window.

I. Click the Distribution Button

Click the Distribution button to open the Sales Transaction Distribution Entry window.

J. Verify the General Ledger Account Distributions

The software automatically distributes amounts from the transaction to general ledger accounts based on information on file for the customer.

The debit amount is either posted to the allowance for uncollectible accounts or to bad debt expense, depending upon the company's accounting policy. The credit amount is posted to accounts receivable.

Click the Show button to display detailed general ledger account information for each posting account.

If the account distributions are correct, close the window.

If the account distributions are not correct, correct the distributions and click the OK button to return to the Receivables Transaction Entry window.

K. Review the Receivables Transaction Entry Window for Completeness and Accuracy

Before the write-off is posted, most errors can be corrected by clicking the box with the error and making the correction. Certain boxes cannot be changed after they are originally completed. Errors in these boxes can only be corrected by deleting the transaction and entering the transaction again.

➤ *Review the Receivables Transaction Entry window for completeness and accuracy. If you find an error while reviewing the window, click the box with the error and make corrections.*

➤ *If the box with the error cannot be accessed or changed, click the Delete button and click Delete again when asked if you are sure that you want to delete this document. Enter the transaction again by returning to step B.*

L. Post the Write-off Transaction

➤ *After you are satisfied with all of the data in the Receivables Transaction Entry window, click the Post button to post the account receivable write-off.*

Transaction Review

After clicking the Post button in the Receivables Transaction Entry window, you can determine if the transaction has been posted to the subsidiary records by completing the steps that follow. Recall that the transaction has not yet been posted to the general ledger.

➤ *Click Sales ➔ Transaction by Document (I) to open the Receivables Transaction Inquiry - Document window.*

Posted receivables transactions by document are shown in the scrolling window of the Receivables Transaction Inquiry - Document window. All write-off transactions contain the letters "CR" in the Type box of the scrolling window.

➤ *Click once on the line containing the write-off transaction you want to review. With the selected invoice highlighted, move the mouse pointer over the Document Number description field until the pointer turns into a hand.*

➤ *When the hand appears, click once on the Document Number description field to zoom to the Receivables Transaction Inquiry Zoom window for the selected write-off transaction.*

The window that appears is a replica of the Receivables Transaction Entry window for the selected transaction. It is not possible to change information through the inquiry window. You can review the account distributions for the transaction by clicking the Distribution button. You can also determine what outstanding invoice(s) the write-off transaction has been applied to by clicking the Apply button.

➤ *Close the Receivables Transaction Inquiry Zoom window and the Receivables Transaction Inquiry - Document window.*

Error Correction After Posting the Transaction

If you discover an error after posting a write-off transaction, refer to Appendix A.

Receive a Miscellaneous Cash Receipt

Overview

The Bank Transaction Entry window is used to process and record a miscellaneous cash receipt. Examples of miscellaneous cash receipts are the receipt of loan proceeds and the sale of a fixed asset. When the Bank Transaction Entry window is posted, no subsidiary records are affected. Later, when the transaction is posted to the general ledger, cash is debited. Other accounts may also be debited, depending on the nature of the transaction. The credit amount of the transaction is posted to either a liability, miscellaneous revenue, or an asset account, depending on the nature of the transaction. **Note: If the miscellaneous cash receipt is from the sale of a fixed asset, perform the procedures as stated on page 144 to retire the fixed asset.**

Quick Reference Table

Step	Box or Other Location	Procedure
A	Navigation Pane buttons	Click *Financial* ➔ *Bank Transactions (T)*.
B	Option	Select "Enter Receipt" as the option.
C	Type	Accept "Check" as the default cash receipt type or select "Cash".
D	Transaction Date	Review the default transaction date and change if necessary.
E	Checkbook ID	Select the Checkbook ID.
F	Rcvd From	Type the name of the company or person from whom the miscellaneous cash was received.
G	Description	Type a description of the miscellaneous cash receipt, including the name entered in the "Rcvd From" box.
H	Amount	Type the amount of the miscellaneous cash receipt.
I	Show button	Click the Show button to reveal the general ledger distribution lines.
J	Cash Account lines in the scrolling window	Accept the contents of all boxes in the cash account portion of the scrolling window.
K	Remainder of the scrolling window	Complete the remaining general ledger distribution lines in the scrolling window.
L	Bank Transaction Entry window	Review the Bank Transaction Entry window for completeness and accuracy.
M	Post button	Post the miscellaneous cash receipt.

Note: You must also record the bank deposit. See pages 48-51.

Receive a Miscellaneous Cash Receipt
Dynamics Window

Bank Transaction Entry Window
Financial → Bank Transactions (T) (A)

(L)

Bank Transaction Entry					_ □ ✕

File (M) dit   Tools   View   Help   sa Jackson Supply Company 2/1/2010

Post   Clear

Option:	Enter Receipt (B) ▾		Type:	Check (C) ▾

Transaction Date	2/1/2010 (D) ▦ →	
Checkbook ID	OHIO (E) 🔍▯	
Currency ID		Rcvd From	Schrauben Brothers (F)
Number	RCT000000001	Description	Misc. rev.-Schrauben Bros (G)
Card Name		Amount	(H) $600.00

Account 🔍 →	Debit	Credit	⇥ ⇤ ⌃
Description	Originating Debit	Originating Credit	⌄ (I)
Distribution Reference			
10100	$600.00	$0.00	
Cash - General Account (J)			
32000	$0.00	$600.00	
Miscellaneous Income (K)			

	Total	$600.00	$600.00
	Difference		$0.00

Receive a Miscellaneous Cash Receipt
Detailed Instructions

A. Click *Financial → Bank Transactions (T)*

> ➤ *Click Financial → Bank Transactions (T) to open the Bank Transaction Entry window.*

B. Select "Enter Receipt" as the Option

> ➤ *Select "Enter Receipt" from the Option drop-down list.*

C. Accept "Check" as the Default Cash Receipt Type or Select "Cash"

> ➤ *Press [Return] to accept "Check" as the receipt type or use the drop-down list to select "Cash". Credit card receipts are not covered in this project.*

D. Review the Default Transaction Date and Change if Necessary

> The correct date in the Transaction Date box is the date the cash was received.

> ➤ *If the date of the miscellaneous cash receipt transaction is different than the date shown, type the correct date.*

E. Select the Checkbook ID

> ➤ *Select the Checkbook ID of the bank account where the funds will be deposited.*

F. Type the Name of the Company or Person from Whom the Miscellaneous Cash was Received

> The Rcvd (Received) From box is used to type the name of the company or person from whom the miscellaneous cash was received.

> ➤ *Type the name of the company or person from whom the miscellaneous cash was received.*

G. Type a Description of the Miscellaneous Cash Receipt, Including the Name Entered in the "Rcvd From" Box

Information typed in the Description box will appear in various *Microsoft Dynamics GP* reports.

 Type a brief description of the miscellaneous cash receipt, including the name you typed in the "Rcvd From" box. For example, for the sale of equipment to Brown & Company, type [Equipment sale - Brown & Co.].

H. Type the Amount of the Miscellaneous Cash Receipt

 Type the amount of the miscellaneous cash receipt.

I. Click the Show Button to Reveal the General Ledger Distribution Lines

Before the miscellaneous cash receipt can be posted, it must first be distributed to general ledger accounts using the scrolling window in the bottom half of the Bank Transaction Entry window. The Show button reveals descriptions of the general ledger accounts.

 Click the Show button to reveal detailed general ledger distribution lines in the scrolling window.

J. Accept the Contents of all Boxes in the Cash Account Portion of the Scrolling Window

The software automatically completes the following three boxes for the cash portion of the transaction, depending on the Checkbook ID selected in step E: Account, Debit, and Description. You cannot change any of this information.

 Either move through all boxes in the cash portion of the scrolling window, or click the Account box for the next general ledger account to be entered.

K. Complete the Remaining General Ledger Distribution Lines in the Scrolling Window

The remaining lines in the scrolling window are used to enter the remaining debit and credit portions of the miscellaneous cash receipt transaction.

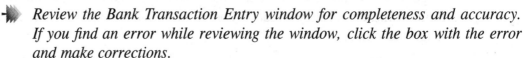 *Select the next general ledger account using the Account lookup button. Type the debit or credit amount for the selected account in the Debit or Credit box. Repeat this step until all general ledger accounts and amounts for the transaction have been entered. Before the transaction can be posted, the amount in the Difference box must be zero (debits equal credits).*

L. Review the Bank Transaction Entry Window for Completeness and Accuracy

Before the miscellaneous cash receipt is posted, most errors can be corrected by clicking the box with the error and making the correction. You can also click the Clear button to start over and enter the transaction again.

➡ *Review the Bank Transaction Entry window for completeness and accuracy. If you find an error while reviewing the window, click the box with the error and make corrections.*

➡ *If the box with the error cannot be accessed or changed, click the Clear button. Enter the transaction again by returning to step B.*

M. Post the Miscellaneous Cash Receipt

➡ *After you are satisfied with all of the data in the Bank Transaction Entry window, click the Post button to post the miscellaneous cash receipt.*

Transaction Review

Because a miscellaneous cash receipt does not affect any subsidiary records, you will not be able to review the transaction yet. Recall that the transaction has not yet been posted to the general ledger.

Error Correction After Posting a Transaction

If you discover an error after posting a miscellaneous cash receipt transaction, refer to Appendix A.

This page is intentionally blank.

Make a Bank Deposit

Overview

The Bank Deposit Entry window is used to record deposits into a company's bank account. After a bank deposit is posted through this window, the deposit is recorded in *Microsoft Dynamics GP's* bank reconciliation module and will appear as an increase in cash for the next bank reconciliation prepared. No entry is made to the general ledger because no transaction occurs.

Quick Reference Table

Step	Box or Other Location	Procedure
A	Navigation Pane buttons	Click *Financial* ➔ *Bank Deposits (T)*.
B	Deposit Date	Review the deposit date and change if necessary.
C	Checkbook ID	Select the checkbook ID of the depository bank.
D	"Dep." check boxes	Select each cash receipt included in the deposit.
E	Deposit Amount	Review the total deposit amount for accuracy.
F	Post	Click the Post button.

Make a Bank Deposit
Dynamics Window

Bank Deposit Entry Window
Financial → Bank Deposits (T) **A**

Make a Bank Deposit
Detailed Instructions

A. Click *Financial* → *Bank Deposits (T)*

 Click Financial → Bank Deposits (T) to open the Bank Deposit Entry window.

B. Review the Deposit Date and Change if Necessary

The default deposit date is the current date.

 Review the deposit date. If it is not correct, type the correct date.

C. Select the Checkbook ID of the Depository Bank

 Use the Checkbook ID lookup button to select the bank account where the funds will be deposited.

D. Select Each Cash Receipt Included in the Deposit

The scrolling window at the bottom of the Bank Deposit Entry window contains a list of all undeposited cash receipts. Each receipt has an adjacent check box on the left side of the scrolling window. This box must be checked in order to include a cash receipt in the deposit.

 If all cash receipts are included in the deposit, click the Mark All button at the top of the scrolling window.

 If only certain cash receipts are deposited, click the check box next to each cash receipt being deposited.

E. Review the Total Deposit Amount for Accuracy

The Deposit Amount box contains a running total of all cash receipts selected in step D. The amount in this box should match the total deposited into the bank account.

 Review the total deposit amount for accuracy. If there are errors, correct them before continuing.

F. Click the Post Button

 Click the Post button to post the bank deposit to the bank reconciliation module.

This page is intentionally blank.

EXPENDITURES CYCLE ACTIVITIES

Expenditures Cycle Activities:

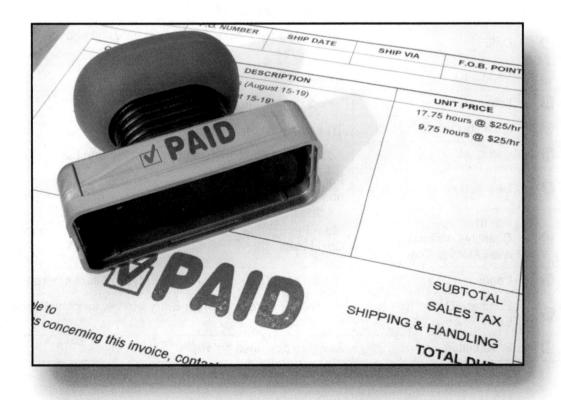

Prepare a Purchase Order

Overview

The Purchase Order Entry window is used to prepare purchase orders for the purchase of both inventory and non-inventory items. No entry (posting) is made to the subsidiary records or general ledger after a purchase order is saved because a liability does not yet exist.

Quick Reference Table

Step	Box or Other Location	Procedure
A	Navigation Pane buttons	Click *Purchasing* → *Purchase Order Entry (T)*.
B	Type	Accept Standard as the purchase order type.
C	PO Number	Accept the default purchase order number or type the correct purchase order number.
D	Date	Review the default purchase order date and change if necessary.
E	Vendor ID	Select the Vendor ID.
F	Item	Select or type the item number ordered.
G	Quantity Ordered	Type the quantity ordered.
H	Unit Cost	Accept the default unit cost or type the correct unit cost.
I	Description	For inventory items, accept the default description; for non-inventory items, type the description of the item ordered.
J	Site ID, Quantity Canceled, and Extended Cost	Move through the Site ID, Quantity Canceled, and Extended Cost boxes.
K	Various	Repeat steps F through J for each type of item ordered.
L	Purchase Order Entry window	Review the Purchase Order Entry window for completeness and accuracy.
M	Save button	Save the purchase order.

Prepare a Purchase Order
Dynamics Window

Purchase Order Entry Window
Purchasing → *Purchase Order Entry (T)* (A)

(L)

Purchase Order Entry [_] [□] [X]

File (M) dit   Tools   View   Options   Help   sa Jackson Supply Company 2/1/2010

💾 **Save** | Blanket | Actio̱ns ▼ |

Type: Standard (B) ▼   [_] Hold   **Vendor ID**   [_____] (E) 🔍 🗋 →
PO Number   [_____] (C) 🔍 🗋   **Name**   [_____]
Buyer ID   [_____]   🔍 🗋   Currency ID   [_____]
Date   2/1/2010 (D)   ▦ →
[_] Allow Sales Documents Commitments

Line	Item (🔍 🗋 →)	U of M 🔍	Quantity Ordered 🗋 🗐	Unit Cost	⋀
Description		Site ID 🔍 🗋	Quantity Canceled	Extended Cost	⋁
0 (I)	(F)	(J)	(J) (G) 0.00	(H) $0.00	⋀
			0.00	(J) $0.00	
(K) {					
					⋁

	Subtotal $0.00
Remaining PO Subtotal $0.00	Trade Discount $0.00
	Freight $0.00 →
	Miscellaneous $0.00 →
Tax Schedule ID [_____] 🔍 🗋	Tax $0.00 →
Comment ID [_____] 🔍 🗋 →	Total $0.00

|◀ ◀ ▶ ▶| PO Number ▼   PO Status New   Revision 0   🗇 ⑦

Prepare a Purchase Order
Detailed Instructions

A. Click *Purchasing → Purchase Order Entry (T)*

➧ *Click Purchasing → Purchase Order Entry (T) to access the Purchase Order Entry window.*

B. Accept Standard as the Purchase Order Type

➧ *The default for the Type box is Standard. Press* [Return] *to accept the default.*

C. Accept the Default Purchase Order Number or Type the Correct Purchase Order Number

The software automatically assigns the next sequential purchase order number in the PO Number box.

➧ *Accept the default purchase order number or type the correct purchase order number.*

D. Review the Default Purchase Order Date and Change if Necessary

➧ *If the purchase order date is different than the date shown, type the correct date.*

E. Select the Vendor ID

➧ *Use the adjacent lookup button to select the vendor ID.*

F. Select or Type the Item Number Ordered

For inventory items, the Item lookup button is used to select the item ordered from a list of items commonly purchased from the selected vendor.

➧ *For an inventory item ordered, use the Item lookup button to select the item number ordered.*

For non-inventory items, *Microsoft Dynamics GP* does not keep a record of item numbers, descriptions, and costs for items commonly purchased from each vendor. This information must be typed when preparing each purchase order.

➧ *For a non-inventory item ordered, type the vendor's item number.*

G. Type the Quantity Ordered

 Type the quantity ordered.

H. Accept the Default Unit Cost or Type the Correct Unit Cost

For inventory items, *Microsoft Dynamics GP* automatically completes the Unit Cost box using information on file for the selected vendor and inventory item. For non-inventory items, the unit cost must be typed during the preparation of the purchase order.

 For inventory items, accept the unit cost or type the correct unit cost if it is different from the default.

 For non-inventory items, type the unit cost.

I. For Inventory Items, Accept the Default Description;
For Non-inventory Items, Type the Description of the Item Ordered

For inventory items, the software automatically completes the Description box using information on file for the selected inventory item. For non-inventory items, the description must be typed during the preparation of the purchase order.

 For inventory items, accept the description or type a new description.

 For non-inventory items, type the vendor description of the item ordered.

J. Move Through the Site ID, Quantity Canceled, and Extended Cost Boxes

The Site ID, Quantity Canceled, and Extended Cost boxes are already filled with the correct default information. In order to enter the Item box for the next item ordered, however, you need to move through these three boxes.

 Press [Return] *repeatedly until the cursor reaches the next blank Item box.*

K. Repeat Steps F through J for Each Type of Item Ordered

 Continue entering information for each type of item ordered.

For non-inventory items, the software automatically updates the Tax box with the appropriate tax amount for the purchase order total.

L. Review the Purchase Order Entry Window for Completeness and Accuracy

Before the purchase order is saved, most errors can be corrected by clicking the box with the error and making the correction. Certain boxes cannot be changed after they are originally completed. Errors in these boxes can only be corrected by deleting the purchase order window and entering the purchase order again.

➤ *Review the Purchase Order Entry window for completeness and accuracy. If you find an error while reviewing the window, click the box with the error and make corrections.*

➤ *If the box with the error cannot be accessed or changed, click the Delete button and click Delete again when asked if you are sure that you want to delete this record. Enter the purchase order again by returning to step B.*

M. Save the Purchase Order

➤ *After you are satisfied with all of the data in the Purchase Order Entry window, click the Save button to save the purchase order.*

Purchase Order Review

After a purchase order is saved, you can determine if it has been included in the system by completing the steps that follow. Because no transaction occurred, no posting entry is made to either the subsidiary records or to the general ledger.

➤ *Click Purchasing → Purchase Order Documents (I) to open the Purchase Order Processing Document Inquiry window.*

➤ *Click the box to the left of "Open Purchase Orders" in the middle of the window.*

➤ *Click the Redisplay button. The scrolling window shows a list of open purchase orders.*

➤ *Locate the purchase order you want to review and click once on its line. Zoom on the PO Number description field to open the Purchase Order Inquiry Zoom window for the selected purchase order.*

The window that appears is a replica of the Purchase Order Entry window for the selected purchase order. By clicking the Show button, you can review details for each item in the purchase order. It is not possible to change information through the inquiry window.

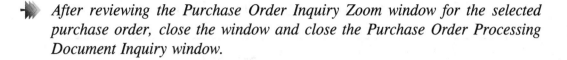

➤ *After reviewing the Purchase Order Inquiry Zoom window for the selected purchase order, close the window and close the Purchase Order Processing Document Inquiry window.*

Error Correction After Saving a Purchase Order

If you discover an error after saving a purchase order, refer to Appendix A.

Receive Goods from a Purchase Order

Overview

The Receivings Transaction Entry window is used to process and record the receipt of goods from an open purchase order. After the Receivings Transaction Entry window is posted, the accounts payable subsidiary records are updated automatically for the effects of the transaction. If inventory was received, the perpetual inventory records are also adjusted accordingly. Later, when the transaction is posted to the general ledger, an asset or expense account is debited and accounts payable is credited.

Quick Reference Table

Step	Box or Other Location	Procedure
Ⓐ	Navigation Pane buttons	Click *Purchasing* ➔ *Receivings Transaction Entry (T)*.
Ⓑ	Type	Select Shipment/Invoice as the type of receipt.
Ⓒ	Vendor Doc. No.	Type the vendor's invoice number.
Ⓓ	Date	Review the default receipt date and change if necessary.
Ⓔ	Vendor ID	Select the Vendor ID.
Ⓕ	PO Number	Select the purchase order number for which the shipment is received.
Ⓖ	Auto-Rcv button	Click the Auto-Rcv button.*
Ⓗ	Quantity Shipped **	Review the quantity shipped for each item ordered and change if necessary.
Ⓘ	Quantity Invoiced**	Review the quantity invoiced for each item ordered and change if necessary.
Ⓙ	Various**	Enter receipt information for goods received from other open purchase orders, if applicable.
Ⓚ	Receive button**	Click the Receive button.
Ⓛ	Payment Terms	Review the payment terms and change if necessary.
Ⓜ	Tax	Enter the sales tax amount, if applicable.
Ⓝ	Distributions button	Click the Distributions button and verify the general ledger account distributions.
Ⓞ	Receivings Transaction Entry window	Review the Receivings Transaction Entry window for completeness and accuracy.
Ⓟ	Post button	Post the receipt of goods.

  * This opens the Select Purchase Order Items window.
  ** Steps H-K are in the Select Purchase Order Items window.

Receive Goods from a Purchase Order
Dynamics Windows

Receivings Transaction Entry Window
Purchasing → Receivings Transaction Entry (T) **A**

O

Receivings Transaction Entry

File   Edit   Tools   View   Options   Help **P**   **G**   sa Jackson Supply Company 2/1/2010

💾 **Save**   ✖ Delete   Void   Post   Auto-Rcv   Reports

Type:	Shipment/Invoice **B** ▾	**Vendor ID**	**E** 🔍🗋→
Receipt No.	🔍🗋	Name	
Vendor Doc. No.	**C**	Currency ID	
Date	2/1/2010 **D** 🔳→		
Batch ID	🔍🗋→		

PO Number 🔍🗋 Item ⓘ🔍🗋→ Qty Shipped 🔲 Unit Cost →≫
U of M 🔍 Site ID 🔍🗋 Quantity Ordered 🗋 Quantity Invoiced Extended Cost ≫
Description **F** Previously Shipped Previously Invoiced

1099 Amount	$0.00	Subtotal	$0.00
Payment Terms	🔍🗋→ **L**	Trade Discount	$0.00
Landed Cost Func. Total	→	Freight	$0.00 →
		Miscellaneous	$0.00 →
		Tax	$0.00 → **M**
Purch Addr Tax Sched	🔍🗋	Total	$0.00

Landed Cost **N** Distributions   User-Defined

◀◀ ◀ ▶ ▶▶   Receipt Number ▾

Select Purchase Order Items Window

Select Purchase Order Items

File   Edit   Tools   Options   Help   sa Jackson Supply Company 2/1/2010

Vendor ID	AMER0001	Currency ID	
Vendor Name	American Linen Supply	Receipt Number	RCT7518
Sort By:	PO / Items ▾	Display:	⦿ All ◯ Marked

Mark All   Unmark All

🔒 · On Hold

Mark All   Unmark All

		PO Number	Item		Qty Shipped	≫
⊟	AMER0001	Site ID	U of M	Qty Ordered	Qty Invoiced	≫
⊞	5875	Line	Item Description		Unit Cost	
⊞	5876	☐ 5875	101		0 **H**	
		MAIN	1	10	0 **I**	
		1	Bath towels · 100 pack		$175.00	
		☑ 5876	108		25 **H**	
		MAIN	1	25	25 **I**	
		1	Blanket		$17.50	
J		☑ 5876	104		15	
		MAIN	1	15	15	
		2	Standard sheet set		$23.50	

K Receive   Cancel

Receive Goods from a Purchase Order
Detailed Instructions

> **Warning:** Because error correction for receiving goods from a purchase order is extremely complicated, review the Receivings Transaction Entry window carefully before clicking the Post button. Error correction is discussed in Appendix A.

A. Click *Purchasing* → *Receivings Transaction Entry (T)*

➤ *Click Purchasing → Receivings Transaction Entry (T) to open the Receivings Transaction Entry window.*

B. Select Shipment/Invoice as the Type of Receipt

The Receivings Transaction Entry window is used to record the receipt of goods with or without an invoice. However, the only way a receipt of goods transaction is recorded as a liability is to record a shipment with an invoice. For this project, assume that all shipments include an invoice.

➤ *Use the Type drop-down list to select **Shipment/Invoice** as the type of receipt.*

C. Type the Vendor's Invoice Number

➤ *Type the vendor's invoice number in the Vendor Doc. No. box.*

D. Review the Default Receipt Date and Change if Necessary

➤ *If the date of the receipt of goods transaction is different than the date shown, type the correct date.*

E. Select the Vendor ID

➤ *Use the adjacent lookup button to select the vendor ID.*

F. Select the Purchase Order Number for Which the Shipment is Received

The PO Number lookup button is used to access a list of all open purchase orders.

 Use the PO Number lookup button to select the purchase order for which the shipment is received.

G. Click the Auto-Rcv Button

The Auto-Rcv button is used to automatically receive and invoice all items from the purchase order selected in step F. After clicking the Auto-Rcv button, the Select Purchase Order Items window opens.

Click the Auto-Rcv button to open the Select Purchase Order Items window.

The lower left part of the Select Purchase Order Items window displays all open purchase orders for the selected vendor. The lower right portion of the window displays the detailed items that are part of each open purchase order. There should be a check mark next to each item that is part of the purchase order number selected in step F. Notice that all other items that are not part of the purchase order number selected in step F are not checked.

H. Review the Quantity Shipped for Each Item Ordered and Change if Necessary

After the Auto-Rcv button is clicked in step G, the software automatically completes the Quantity Shipped box for each item in the selected purchase order using the quantity ordered on the original purchase order. If the quantity received differs from the quantity ordered for any item, you must change the amount in that item's Quantity Shipped box.

Review the Quantity Shipped box for each item shipped from the selected purchase order. If a different quantity was received than was ordered, type the correct quantity received.

I. Review the Quantity Invoiced for Each Item Ordered and Change if Necessary

Microsoft Dynamics GP automatically completes the Quantity Invoiced box for each item in the selected purchase order using the quantity ordered on the original purchase order. If the quantity billed by the vendor differs from the quantity ordered for any item, you must change the amount in that item's Quantity Invoiced box.

➤ *Review the Quantity Invoiced box for each item in the selected purchase order. If a different quantity was billed than was ordered, type the correct quantity billed.*

J. Enter Receipt Information for Goods Received from Other Open Purchase Orders, if Applicable

Vendors frequently ship goods from more than one purchase order in the same shipment. The Select Purchase Order Items window allows you to enter the receipt of goods from other open purchase orders.

➤ *If there were no goods shipped from other open purchase orders, skip to step K.*

➤ *If goods were received from other open purchase orders, click the check box next to each item received and repeat steps H and I for each item received.*

K. Click the Receive Button

➤ *After all receipt information is entered correctly, click the Receive button. This returns the screen to the Receivings Transaction Entry Window.*

L. Review the Payment Terms and Change if Necessary

The software automatically completes the Payment Terms box using default information on file for the selected vendor.

➤ *Compare the contents of the Payment Terms box with the payment terms on the vendor's invoice and change the terms if necessary using the adjacent lookup button.*

M. Enter the Sales Tax Amount, if Applicable

➤ *If the vendor's invoice includes sales tax, type the sales tax amount in the Tax box. This opens the Receivings Tax Summary Entry window. Select the purchases option in the Tax Details ID box (PURCH, for example) and then click OK.*

➤ *If there is no sales tax, skip to step N.*

N. Click the Distributions Button and Verify the General Ledger Account Distributions

Microsoft Dynamics GP automatically distributes amounts from the transaction to general ledger accounts based upon information on file for the selected vendor.

➤ *Click the Distributions button to view the Purchasing Distribution Entry window.*

➤ *Click the Show button to reveal the general ledger account names.*

➤ *Make changes as necessary and click the OK button to return to the Receivings Transaction Entry window.*

O. Review the Receivings Transaction Entry Window for Completeness and Accuracy

As discussed earlier, error correction after posting the Receivings Transaction Entry window is extremely complicated. Therefore, you should review the window carefully before posting.

Before the transaction is posted, most errors can be corrected by clicking the box with the error and making the correction. Certain boxes cannot be changed after they are originally completed. Errors in these boxes can only be corrected by deleting the transaction and entering the transaction again.

➤ *Review the Receivings Transaction Entry window for completeness and accuracy. If you find an error while reviewing the window, click the box with the error and make corrections.*

➤ *If the box with the error cannot be accessed or changed, click the Delete button and click Delete again when asked if you are sure that you want to delete this record. Enter the transaction again by returning to step B.*

P. Post the Receipt of Goods

> *After you are satisfied with all of the data in the Receivings Transaction Entry window, click the Post button to post the receipt of goods.*

Transaction Review

After clicking the Post button in the Receivings Transaction Entry window, you can determine if the transaction has been posted to the subsidiary records by completing the steps that follow. Recall that the purchase has not yet been posted to the general ledger.

> *Click Purchasing → Transaction by Vendor (I) to open the Payables Transaction Inquiry - Vendor window.*

> *Use the Vendor ID lookup button to select the vendor from the transaction you want to review.*

> *Locate the invoice number from the transaction you want to review and click once on its line.*

> *Zoom on the Document Number description field.*

> *After reviewing the Payables Transaction Entry Zoom window for the selected transaction, close the window and close the Payables Transaction Inquiry - Vendor window.*

Error Correction After Posting a Transaction

If you discover an error after posting a receipt of goods transaction, refer to Appendix A.

This page is intentionally blank.

Pay a Vendor's Outstanding Invoice

Overview

Payments of vendors' outstanding invoices are processed and recorded using the Payables Manual Payment Entry and the Apply Payables Documents windows. For invoices that are processed and paid on the same day, see pages 74-79.

After the windows are posted, the accounts payable subsidiary records are updated. Later, when the transaction is posted to the general ledger, accounts payable is debited, cash is credited, and purchase discounts is also credited, if applicable.

Quick Reference Table

Step	Box or Other Location	Procedure
A	Navigation Pane buttons	Click *Purchasing* → *Manual Payments (T)*.
B	Date	Review the default payment date and change if necessary.
C	Vendor ID	Select the Vendor ID.
D	Payment Method	Select the type of payment.
E	Document No.	Review the default document number and change if necessary.
F	Amount	Type the payment amount.
G	Apply button	Click the Apply button.
H	Check boxes (Apply Payables Documents window)	Click the Show button and select the invoice(s) to which the cash disbursement is being applied.
I	OK button (Apply Payables Documents window)	Click the OK button in the Apply Payables Documents window.
J	Distribution button	Click the Distribution button.
K	Payables Transaction Entry Distribution window (not shown)	Click the Show button and verify the general ledger account distributions.
L	Payables Manual Payment Entry window	Review the Payables Manual Payment Entry window for completeness and accuracy.
M	Post button	Post the cash disbursement.

Pay a Vendor's Outstanding Invoice
Dynamics Windows

Payables Manual Payment Entry Window
Purchasing → Manual Payments (T) **A**

Apply Payables Documents Window

Pay a Vendor's Outstanding Invoice
Detailed Instructions

A. Click *Purchasing → Manual Payments (T)*

➤ *Click Purchasing → Manual Payments (T) to access the Payables Manual Payment Entry window.*

B. Review the Default Payment Date and Change if Necessary

➤ *If the payment date is different than the date shown, type the correct date.*

C. Select the Vendor ID

➤ *Use the adjacent lookup button to select the vendor ID.*

D. Select the Type of Payment

➤ *The default payment type is Check. Press [Return] to accept Check or click the Cash radio button for a payment made in cash.* Credit card payments are not covered in this project.

E. Review the Default Document Number and Change if Necessary

The software automatically assigns the next sequential document number. For checks, the document number is the next sequential check number. For cash payments, the software assigns the next sequential payment number.

➤ *Review the default document number. If it is not correct, type the correct document number.*

F. Type the Payment Amount

➤ *Type the payment amount.*

G. Click the Apply Button

Cash disbursements need to be applied to outstanding invoices. The application process is done through the Apply Payables Documents window, which can be accessed from the Payables Manual Payment Entry window. The Apply Payables Documents window is shown on the bottom of page 69.

➤ *Click the Apply button to access the Apply Payables Documents window.*

H. Click the Show Button and Select the Invoice(s) to Which the Cash Disbursement is being Applied

The Apply Payables Documents window is similar to the Apply Sales Documents window, which was described in the Receive Goods on a Sales Return section on pages 22-28.

➤ *Click the Show button to show the detail lines for each invoice in the scrolling window.*

➤ *Locate the invoice(s) to which the cash disbursement is being applied. To apply the cash disbursement to an invoice, click the adjacent check box. When the cash disbursement is fully applied, the amount in the Unapplied Amount box will be zero.*

I. Click the OK Button in the Apply Payables Documents Window

➤ *When the cash disbursement has been fully applied, click the OK button to save the information and to return to the Payables Manual Payment Entry window.*

J. Click the Distribution Button

➤ *Click the Distribution button to access the Payables Transaction Entry Distribution window.*

K. Click the Show Button and Verify the General Ledger Account Distributions

Microsoft Dynamics GP automatically distributes amounts from the transaction to general ledger accounts based on information on file for the selected vendor and bank account.

➤ *Click the Show button to show the detail lines for each general ledger account in the scrolling window.*

➤ *Make changes if necessary in the Payables Transaction Entry Distribution window and then click the OK button.*

L. Review the Payables Manual Payment Entry Window for Completeness and Accuracy

Before a transaction is posted, most errors can be corrected by clicking the box with the error and making the correction. Certain boxes cannot be changed after they are originally completed. Errors in these boxes can only be corrected by deleting the transaction and entering the transaction again.

➤ *Review the window for completeness and accuracy. If you find an error while reviewing the window, click the box with the error and make corrections.*

➤ *If the box with the error cannot be accessed or changed, click the Delete button and click Delete again when asked if you are sure that you want to delete this record. Enter the transaction again by returning to step B.*

M. Post the Cash Disbursement

➤ *After you are satisfied with all of the data in the Payables Manual Payment Entry window, click the Post button to post the cash disbursement.*

Transaction Review

After clicking the Post button in the Payables Manual Payment Entry window, you can determine if the transaction has been posted to the subsidiary records by completing the steps that follow. Recall that the transaction has not yet been posted to the general ledger.

➤ *Click Purchasing → Transaction by Vendor (I) to open the Payables Transaction Inquiry - Vendor Window.*

➤ *Use the Vendor ID lookup button to select the vendor from the cash disbursement transaction just posted.*

➤ *Locate the line containing the cash disbursement just posted and click once on the line. Hint: The letters "PMT" appear in the Type box and the cash disbursement amount appears in the Original Amount box.*

➤ *Zoom on the Document Number description field to access the Payables Payments Zoom window for the selected cash disbursement. When you are done reviewing the transaction, close the window and then close the Payables Transaction Inquiry - Vendor window.*

Error Correction After Posting the Transaction

If you discover an error after posting the payment of a vendor's outstanding invoice, refer to Appendix A.

Purchase Goods or Services
Without a Purchase Order

Overview

The Payables Transaction Entry window is used to process and record a vendor's invoice for goods or services purchased without a purchase order, such as utility charges or legal fees. If payment of the invoice is made on the date the invoice is recorded, the payment can also be recorded in the Payables Transaction Entry window at the same time.

The posted transaction updates the vendor subsidiary records. Later, when the transaction is posted to the general ledger, an expense or asset account is debited and accounts payable or cash is credited, depending upon whether payment is made on the same day.

Quick Reference Table

Step	Box or Other Location	Procedure
Ⓐ	Navigation Pane buttons	Click *Purchasing* ➔ *Transaction Entry (T)*.
Ⓑ	Description	Type a description of the transaction.
Ⓒ	Doc. Date	Review the default transaction date and change if necessary.
Ⓓ	Vendor ID	Select the Vendor ID.
Ⓔ	Payment Terms	Review the payment terms and change if necessary.
Ⓕ	Document Number	Type the vendor invoice number.
Ⓖ	Shipping Method	Accept or select the shipping method, if applicable.
Ⓗ	Purchases	Type the purchase amount from the invoice.
Ⓘ	Check	Type the amount of the check, if applicable.
Ⓙ	Distributions button	Click the Distributions button.
Ⓚ	Payables Transaction Entry Distribution window (not shown)	Verify the general ledger account distributions.
Ⓛ	Payables Transaction Entry window	Review the Payables Transaction Entry window for completeness and accuracy.
Ⓜ	Post button	Post the invoice transaction.

Purchase Goods or Services
Without a Purchase Order
Dynamics Window

Payables Transaction Entry Window
Purchasing → Transaction Entry (T) **A**

L 🖥 **Payables Transaction Entry**   sa Jackson Supply Company 2/1/2010

File   Edit   Tools   Options   **M**

💾 **Save**   ✕ **D**elete   📇 **Post**   🖨 **Pri**nt

Voucher No.	00000000000000031 🔍 📄 ☐ Intercompany	**Batch ID** 🔍 →
Document Type:	Invoice ⌄ **B**	**Doc. Date** 2/1/2010 **C** ▦ →
Description		

Vendor ID **D** 🔍		Currency ID
Name		**Document Number** **F**
Address ID 🔍		P.O. Number
Remit-To ID 🔍		Shipping Method **G** 🔍
Payment Terms **E** 🔍 →		Tax Schedule ID 🔍 →

Purchases **H**	$0.00	1099 Amount	$0.00 →
Trade Discount	$0.00	Cash	$0.00 →
Freight	$0.00	Check **I**	$0.00 →
Miscellaneous	$0.00	Credit Card	$0.00 →
Tax	$0.00 →	Terms Disc Taken	$0.00
Total	$0.00	On Account	$0.00

Apply **J** Distributions   Print Check

⏮ ◀ ▶ ⏭   by Batch ID ⌄   Status Unsaved

Purchase Goods or Services
Without a Purchase Order
Detailed Instructions

A. Click *Purchasing → Transaction Entry (T)*

> ➤ *Click Purchasing → Transaction Entry (T) to access the Payables Transaction Entry window.*

B. Type a Description of the Transaction

> ➤ *Type a brief description of the transaction, for example: "Legal fees — Doud case."*

C. Review the Default Transaction Date and Change if Necessary

The date entered in the Doc. Date box is the date the invoice will be posted to the general ledger. The date entered should represent the date the company incurred the liability. In many cases, the date is the same as the invoice date.

> ➤ *If the transaction date is different than the date shown, type the correct date.*

D. Select the Vendor ID

> ➤ *Use the adjacent lookup button to select the vendor ID.*

E. Review the Payment Terms and Change if Necessary

Microsoft Dynamics GP automatically completes the Payment Terms box using information on file for the selected vendor.

> ➤ *Review the payment terms and change if necessary.*

F. Type the Vendor Invoice Number

> ➤ *Type the vendor invoice number in the Document Number box.*

G. Accept or Select the Shipping Method, if Applicable

If applicable to the selected vendor, the software automatically completes the Shipping Method box using information on file for the selected vendor.

Accept the default shipping method or use the adjacent lookup button to select the shipping method, if applicable.

H. Type the Purchase Amount from the Invoice

The Purchases box is used to type the dollar amount of goods or services from the vendor's invoice.

Type the purchase amount from the invoice.

I. Type the Amount of the Check, if Applicable

If the invoice is being paid on the same date it is entered in the system, you can record the payment simultaneously. Only checks are used in this project.

For an invoice being paid on the same date, type the check amount in the Check box and press [Return]. The Payables Check Entry window appears. Review the information in the window and change it if necessary. When you are done, click the OK button to return to the main window.

J. Click the Distributions Button

Click the Distributions button to open the Payables Transaction Entry Distribution window.

K. Verify the General Ledger Account Distributions

Microsoft Dynamics GP automatically distributes amounts from the transaction to general ledger accounts based upon information on file for the selected vendor. The debit side of the transaction is usually an expense or asset account. The credit side is a liability account (if no payment was entered in step I) or cash (if a cash payment was entered in step I).

Click the Show button to display detailed general ledger account information for each posting account.

If the account distributions are correct, close the window.

If the account distributions are not correct, correct the distributions and click the OK button to save the changes and to return to the Payables Transaction Entry window.

L. Review the Payables Transaction Entry Window for Completeness and Accuracy

Before a transaction is posted, most errors can be corrected by clicking the box with the error and making the correction. Certain boxes cannot be changed after they are originally completed. Errors in these boxes can only be corrected by deleting the transaction and entering the transaction again.

➤ *Review the Payables Transaction Entry window for completeness and accuracy. If you find an error while reviewing the window, click the box with the error and make corrections.*

➤ *If the box with the error cannot be accessed or changed, click the Delete button and click Delete again when asked if you are sure that you want to delete this record. Enter the transaction again by returning to step B.*

M. Post the Invoice Transaction

➤ *After you are satisfied with all of the data in the Payables Transaction Entry window, click the Post button to post the invoice transaction.*

Transaction Review

After clicking the Post button in the Payables Transaction Entry window, you can determine if the transaction has been posted to the subsidiary records by completing the steps that follow. Recall that the transaction has not yet been posted to the general ledger.

➤ *Click Purchasing → Transaction by Vendor (I) to open the Payables Transaction Inquiry - Vendor window.*

➤ *Select the Vendor ID related to the invoice you want to review.*

➤ *Locate the line containing the invoice you want to review and click once on its line.*

➤ *Zoom on the Document Number description field to open the Payables Transaction Entry Zoom window for the selected invoice.*

The window that appears is a replica of the Payables Transaction Entry window for the selected invoice. It is not possible to change information through the inquiry window. You can review the account distributions for the selected invoice by clicking the Distribution button. You can also click the Apply button to review any payments that have been applied to the invoice.

➤ *Close the Payables Transaction Entry Zoom window to return to the Payables Transaction Inquiry - Vendor window.*

➤ *If the invoice was posted and paid on the same day, locate the line containing the payment of the selected invoice and click once on the line.*

➤ *Zoom on the Document Number description field to open the Payables Payments Zoom window for the selected payment.*

➤ *After reviewing the payment, close the Payables Payments Zoom window and the Payables Transaction Inquiry - Vendor window.*

Error Correction After Posting the Transaction

If you discover an error after posting an invoice transaction, refer to Appendix A.

This page is intentionally blank.

PAYROLL CYCLE
AND OTHER ACTIVITIES

Pay Employees

Overview

Several windows are used to process and record payroll: Payroll Transaction Entry, Build Payroll Checks, Calculate Payroll Checks, Print Payroll Checks, and Post Payroll Checks. Because there are several steps involved in the payroll entry process, the windows shown on pages 84 and 85 have sample information entered to help you perform the required steps accurately. After all payroll windows are completed and posted, the employee records are updated. Later, when the transaction is posted to the general ledger, wages and salaries expense and employer's FICA tax expense are debited and cash and payroll withholding liabilities are credited.

Quick Reference Table

(Note: See hints on page 83 before processing payroll – especially #1 about closing each window after completing its requirements.)

Step	Box or Other Location	Procedure
A	Navigation Pane buttons	Click *HR & Payroll* → *Transaction Entry (T)*.
B	Batch ID	Select the Batch ID.
C	Pay Period From and To	Type the beginning and ending pay period dates.
D	Days Worked/ Weeks Worked	Type the number of days or weeks worked during the pay period.
E	Employee ID	Select the Employee ID (hourly employees only).
F	Code	Select the pay code.
G	Amount	Enter the number of regular or overtime hours worked.
H	Next blank Employee ID box	Move the cursor to the next blank Employee ID box.
I	Various	Repeat steps E-H for the selected employee's overtime hours, if applicable.
J	Various	Repeat steps E-I for all remaining hourly employees.
K	Close button	Close the Payroll Transaction Entry window, then click Print and OK.
L	Navigation Pane buttons	Click *HR & Payroll* → *Build Checks (T)*.
M	Pay Period Date From and To	Type the beginning and ending pay period dates.
N	Include Pay Periods	Click the pay period type to be included in the pay run.
O	Salary check box	Click the Salary check box.
P	Select Batches button	Click the Select Batches button, click the appropriate Status box in the Payroll Check Batches window (not shown), and click OK.
Q	Build button	Click the Build button, then click OK in Report Destination window (not shown).
R	Navigation Pane buttons	Click *HR & Payroll* → *Calculate Checks (T)*.
S	OK button	Click the OK button and then click the Cancel button.
T	Navigation Pane buttons	Click *HR & Payroll* → *Print Checks (T)*.
U	Print drop-down list box	Select Checks in Print drop-down list box.
V	Starting Check Number	Review the default starting check number and change if necessary.
W	Check Date	Review the check date and change if necessary.
X	Print button	Click the Print button.
Y	OK button (not shown)	Click OK in the Report Destination window. After all checks are printed on the screen, close the Screen Output window.
Z	Process button	Click the Process button.

Pay Employees
Hints for Processing Payroll

1. There are several windows used in processing payroll. Close each window after you have completed all requirements for the window.
2. Do not enter salaried employees in the Payroll Transaction Entry window. *Microsoft Dynamics GP* automatically processes payroll for salaried employees when you click the Salary check box in the Build Payroll Checks window (Step O).
3. You may need to delete a transaction line in the Payroll Transaction Entry window before the final processing of a transaction. Do so by placing the cursor on the line you want deleted. Select the Delete Row option from the Edit menu on the top of the screen and click Delete after the screen prompt.
4. You will need to add a batch in processing payroll transactions if there is no batch date included in the Batch ID window. This might happen if you discover an error and have to delete a batch before starting over again. To add a Batch ID, do the following:

   ➡ *Click HR & Payroll* ➔ *Batches (T).*
   ➡ *Enter the batch date in the Batch ID box. For example, type* [123109] *for the December 31, 2009 pay date.*
   ➡ *Select Computer Checks in the Origin drop-down list box.*
   ➡ *Click Save and close the window.*

Pay Employees
Dynamics Windows

Payroll Transaction Entry Window
HR & Payroll → Transaction Entry (T) **A**

Payroll Transaction Entry — □ ✕ **K**

File   Edit   Tools   Help   sa Jackson Supply Company 2/1/2010

New Batch   Delete Batch   Print

Batch ID   FEB 15 2010 **B**   🔍

Transaction Defaults

Pay Period From   2/1/20 **C**   Days Worked   **D** 0.00   **Data Entry Options**
         To   2 2010 **C**   Weeks Worked **D** 2.00 **D**   Current Options:
                                                                        No Options   Options...

View Transactions by Order Entered

TRX #	Employee ID	Employee Name	Trx Type	Code	Dept	Amount	Pay Rate
13	10002 **E**	Jorgensen, Kenneth James	Pay Code	HOUR **F**	ACCTG	.67 **G**	$22.00
14	10002 **H** **I**	Jorgensen, Kenneth James	Pay Code	**I**	ACCTG	4.25 **I**	$33.00
15	10003	Phelps, Mark Cameron	Pay Code	HOUR	SHIP	86.67	$14.00
16	10003 **J**	Phelps, Mark Cameron	Pay Code	OVER	SHIP	6.75	$21.00
0						$0.00	$0.00

Batch: FEB 15 2010   2 Employees, 4 Transactions

Build Payroll Checks Window
HR & Payroll → Build Checks (T) **L**

Build Payroll Checks — □ ✕

File   Edit   Tools   Help   sa Jackson Supply Company 2/1/2010

User ID   sa   Build Date   Build Time

Default ID   🔍 →   Description

Type of Pay Run: ⦿ Regular Pay   ◯ Advance Pay

Pay Run Ranges

Pay Period Date: From: 2/1/20 **M**   To: 2/15/2 **M**
Employee Class: ⦿ All   ◯ From: To:
Employee ID: ⦿ All   ◯ From: To:

Include Pay Periods   **Include Automatic Pay Types**

N
☐ Weekly   ☐ Quarterly   **O** ☑ Salary   ☐ Pension   ☐ Earned Income Credit
☐ Biweekly   ☐ Semiannually
☑ Semimonthly ☐ Annually   **For This Pay Period**
☐ Monthly   ☐ Daily/Misc.   Days Worked   Weeks Worked

Include Pay Codes   Include Deductions   Include Benefits   **P** Select Batches

Q Build   Cancel   Remove

Pay Employees
Dynamics Windows, continued

Calculate Payroll Checks Window
HR & Payroll → Calculate Checks (T) **R**

Calculate Payroll Checks				
File	Edit	Tools	Help	2/15/2010 »

User ID	sa
Build Status	Ready
Type of Pay Run	Regular
Build Date	2/15/2010
Build Time	10:27:07 PM
Warnings Exist	No
Errors Exist	No

S OK   Cancel

Print Payroll Checks Window
HR & Payroll → Print Checks (T) **T**

Print Payroll Checks			
File **X**	Tools	Help	2/15/2010 »

Print   Clear

Checkbook ID	OHIO
Name	Ohio National Bank
Print:	Checks **U**
Sort Checks By:	Employee ID
Check Format:	Stub on Top - Continuous
Starting Check Number **V**	513
Check Date	2/15/20 **W**

Post Payroll Checks Window

Post Payroll Checks			
File **Z**	Tools	Help	2/15/2010 »

Process   Clear

Checkbook ID	OHIO
Name	Ohio National Bank
Check Date	2/15/2010
Posting Date	2/15/2010
Process:	Post Checks
Starting Check Number	516

Reprint or Void Range
○ All   ○ From:
         To:

Reason for Voiding

Pay Employees
Detailed Instructions

A. Click *HR & Payroll* → *Transaction Entry (T)*

> *Click HR & Payroll → Transaction Entry (T) to access the Payroll Transaction Entry window.*

B. Select the Batch ID

Payroll transactions are entered in batches rather than on a transaction-by-transaction basis. Many companies create all batches needed for a fiscal year at the beginning of the year to save setup time. For this project, individual batches have already been created for you. All you need to do is to select the appropriate batch.

> *Use the Batch ID lookup button to select the Batch ID that corresponds to the pay period you are processing.*

C. Type the Beginning and Ending Pay Period Dates

The default date in the Pay Period From and To boxes is the User Date. You will need to type the proper beginning and ending pay period dates.

> *Type the beginning and ending pay period dates in the Pay Period From and To boxes.*

D. Type the Number of Days or Weeks Worked During the Pay Period

The Days Worked and Weeks Worked boxes are used to enter the total number of days or weeks in the pay period. The choice of which box to use depends on the type of pay period you are entering. The Days Worked box is used to enter the number of days in a semi-monthly or monthly pay period. The Weeks Worked box is used for weekly and bi-weekly pay periods.

> *Type the number of days or weeks worked in either the Days Worked or Weeks Worked box. Be sure to enter the proper number, considering the decimal point. For example, to enter 11 days in the Days Worked box, type [11.00].*

E. Select the Employee ID (Hourly Employees Only)

The Payroll Transaction Entry window is used to enter regular and overtime hours for all hourly employees. Salaried employees are automatically included in the pay run and do not require any information to be entered in this window.

 Use the Employee ID lookup button to select an hourly employee.

F. Select the Pay Code

The Code box is used to select the type of hours being entered: regular or overtime. For each employee, regular hours are entered first and then overtime hours are entered as a separate line in the window.

 Use the Code box lookup button to select the pay code for the employee's regular or overtime hours. Note: be sure that you are in the Code box for this step and not the Trx Type box.

G. Enter the Number of Regular or Overtime Hours Worked

 Enter the total number of regular or overtime hours worked, either by accepting the default number or typing the correct number. Be sure to use the decimal point appropriately. For example, type [88.00] for 88 hours worked.

H. Move the Cursor to the Next Blank Employee ID Box

 Move to the next blank Employee ID box.

I. Repeat Steps E through H for the Selected Employee's Overtime Hours, if Applicable

If the selected employee has overtime hours for the pay period, you need to enter the Employee ID and other information as a separate line item.

 If the selected employee has overtime hours for the pay period, repeat steps E through H to enter the overtime information.

J. Repeat Steps E through I for All Remaining Hourly Employees

 Continue entering regular and overtime information for each hourly employee to be included in the pay run.

K. Close the Payroll Transaction Entry Window, then Click Print and OK

➤ *After the last hourly employee's regular and overtime information is entered, close the Payroll Transaction Entry window.*

After closing the window, a message appears asking if you want to print a Payroll Transaction Audit report.

➤ *Click Print and then click the OK button to print the report to the screen. Review the information in the report for completeness and accuracy. If you find an error, return to the Payroll Transaction Entry window, select the Batch ID you just entered, and make the necessary corrections.*

L. Click *HR & Payroll → Build Checks (T)*

The next step in the payroll process is to build payroll checks from the information you entered in the Payroll Transaction Entry window.

➤ *Click HR & Payroll → Build Checks (T) to access the Build Payroll Checks window. This window is illustrated on the bottom of page 84.*

M. Type the Beginning and Ending Pay Period Dates

➤ *Type the beginning and ending pay period dates in the Pay Period Date From and To boxes.*

N. Click the Pay Period Type to be Included in the Pay Run

In the lower left portion of the Build Payroll Checks window, there are eight check boxes, each corresponding to a specific pay period type. For example, if a company pays employees twice per month, the pay period is "Semimonthly."

➤ *Click the check box next to the type of pay period the company uses for its employees.*

O. Click the Salary Check Box

As stated in step E, salaried employees are automatically included in a pay run without you having to enter any information. This is accomplished by checking the Salary box in the Build Payroll Checks window.

 Click the Salary check box in the "Include Automatic Pay Types" section of the window.

P. Click the Select Batches Button, Click the Appropriate Status Box in the Payroll Check Batches Window, and Click OK

 Click the Select Batches button in the lower right portion of the Build Payroll Checks window. This opens the Payroll Check Batches window.

 Click the check box in the Status column for the Batch ID that corresponds to the pay run you are building. After clicking this check box, the selected batch changes from "Available" status to "Marked" status.

 Click the OK button to return to the Build Payroll Checks window.

Q. Click the Build Button and then Click OK in the Report Destination Window

 When you are sure that all information in the Build Payroll Checks Window is complete and accurate, click the Build button.

After the Build button is clicked, two progress windows flash across the screen and a Report Destination window opens with the Build Check File Report listed at the top.

 Click the OK button to review the Build Check File Report on the screen for completeness and accuracy. If there are errors, close the Screen Output window and complete the following steps. If there are no errors, close the window and skip to step R.

1. *Click HR & Payroll → Build Checks (T) to open the Build Payroll Checks window.* The window will contain the information you entered when you built the check run.
2. *Click the Remove button and click Remove again when asked if you are sure you want to remove the build.*
3. *Repeat steps M-Q to build the pay checks again with the correct information.*

R. Click *HR & Payroll* → *Calculate Checks (T)*

The next step in the payroll process is to calculate the employees' pay checks, including all appropriate withholdings.

➤ *Click HR & Payroll → Calculate Checks (T) to open the Calculate Payroll Checks window.* This window is shown at the top of page 85.

S. Click the OK Button and then Click the Cancel Button

➤ *Click the OK button to calculate the pay checks.*

After a few progress windows flash across the screen, a Report Destination window appears.

➤ *Click the Cancel button to close the Report Destination window.*

T. Click *HR & Payroll* → *Print Checks (T)*

The next step in the payroll process is to print the pay checks. For this project, you will be printing the checks to the screen.

➤ *Click HR & Payroll → Print Checks (T) to open the Print Payroll Checks window.* This window is shown at the top of page 85.

U. Select Checks in the Print Drop-Down List Box

The Print Payroll Checks window includes a default to use the next check number as an alignment test for a hard copy of the pay checks. You will not be printing a hard copy of paychecks for this project so there is no need to test the alignment.

➤ *Use the Print drop-down list to select "Checks."*

V. Review the Default Starting Check Number and Change if Necessary

➤ *If the first check number to be used in the pay run is different from the default check number in the window, type the correct check number.*

W. Review the Check Date and Change if Necessary

➤ *If the check date is different from the default check date on the window, type the correct check date.*

X. Click the Print Button

➤ *Click the Print button to open the Report Destination window.*

Y. Click OK in the Report Destination Window. After All Checks are Printed on the Screen, Close the Screen Output Window

➤ *Click the OK button in the Report Destination window to print the checks to the screen.* You cannot finish processing the paychecks until the checks are printed to the screen.

➤ *After the last paycheck is printed to the screen, close the Screen Output window.* This will open up the Post Payroll Checks window, which is shown on the bottom of page 85.

Z. Click the Process Button

The final step in the payroll process is to record the paychecks to the payroll module using the Post Payroll Checks window.

➤ *Click the Process button to post the paychecks.* Do not be concerned that the check number in the Starting Check Number box is different from the starting check number for the pay run you are processing. The check number in this window is the check number that will be used in the next pay run. *Note: If you receive a message about vacation and sick pay accruals, click the OK button.*

Transaction Review

After processing payroll checks, you can determine if the underlying transactions have been posted to the employees' subsidiary records by completing the steps that follow. Recall that the transactions have not yet been posted to the general ledger.

➤ *Click HR & Payroll* ➔ *Check History (I) to open the Payroll Check Inquiry window.*

➤ *Use the Employee ID lookup button to select the employee whose payroll check you want to review.*

➤ *Click the Show button.*

➤ *Locate the payroll check you want to review and review the gross pay, withholdings, and net pay amounts.* Unlike most other inquiry windows, you cannot zoom to the original transaction window. However, all pertinent information about the payroll check is available in the inquiry window.

➤ *Close the Payroll Check Inquiry window.*

Error Correction After Posting the Transactions

If you discover an error after posting a pay run, refer to Appendix A.

This page is intentionally blank.

Prepare a General Journal Entry

Overview

The Transaction Entry window is used to process and record a general journal entry. General journal entries are recorded for transactions that do not originate from other transactions cycles. Examples include an annual estimate of bad debt expense and the accrual of federal income taxes.

The posted transaction updates the general ledger by debiting or crediting each account for the amount entered in the Transaction Entry window.

Note: It is essential that you not use the Transaction Entry window for any transaction that affects a subsidiary record because subsidiary records are not updated with this window. An example is a write-off of an uncollectible account receivable.

Quick Reference Table

Step	Box or Other Location	Procedure
A	Navigation Pane buttons	Click *Financial* ➔ *General (T)*.
B	Transaction Date	Review the default journal entry date and change if necessary.
C	Reference	Type a description of the journal entry.
D	Account	Select or type the general ledger account number.
E	Debit / Credit	Type the debit or credit amount for the account selected in step D.*
F	Various	Repeat steps D and E for each account in the journal entry.
G	Difference	Verify that the amount in the Difference box is zero.
H	Show button	Click the Show button.
I	Transaction Entry window	Review the Transaction Entry window for completeness and accuracy.
J	Post button	Post the general journal entry.

* If a default amount is in the Amount box, accept it or type the correct amount.

Prepare a General Journal Entry
Dynamics Window

Transaction Entry Window
Financial → General (T) (A)

(I)

🖳 Transaction Entry					— □ ✕

File   Edit   Tools   View   Help   sa Jackson Supply Company 2/1/2010

💾 **Save**   ✕ **D**elete   ╱ **V**oid   📧 **P**ost   📇 Correct   📋 Copy   🖨

Journal Entry   115 🔍 📄   ☐ Intercompany   Batch ID   🔍 →

Transaction Type: **Transaction Date**   2/1/2010 (B) ▦
◉ Standard   ○ Reversing   Reversing Date

Source Document   GJ   🔍
Reference   (C)
Currency ID   ⌐ ÷ ☐

Co. ID ⌐ ÷ Account	🔍 → Debit	Credit	⌄
Description			⌄
Distribution Reference		Corresp Co. ID	
(D)	(E) $0.00	(E) $0.00	⌃
(F) {			
			⌄
Total	$0.00	$0.00	
	Difference	(G) $0.00	

(H)

|◀ ◀ ▶ ▶| by Batch ID   ⌄   Status   Unposted   📖 ⊚

Prepare a General Journal Entry
Detailed Instructions

A. Click *Financial* → *General (T)*

➤ *Click Financial → General (T) to access the Transaction Entry window.*

B. Review the Default Journal Entry Date and Change if Necessary

➤ *If the journal entry date if different than the date shown, type the correct date.*

C. Type a Description of the Journal Entry

➤ *Type a description of the journal entry in the Reference box, for example: "Y/E accrued interest."*

D. Select or Type the General Ledger Account Number

➤ *Use the Account lookup button to select the general ledger account to be debited or credited or type the account number.*

E. Type the Debit or Credit Amount for the Account Selected in Step D

The Debit and Credit boxes are used to type the amount to be posted to the account selected in step D. You cannot type an amount in both boxes for one account.

➤ *Type the debit or credit amount for the account selected in step D.*

F. Repeat Steps D and E for each Account in the Journal Entry

For second and subsequent accounts, the Debit or Credit box may already contain a default amount. For example, *Microsoft Dynamics GP* usually completes the Credit box with the amount needed to balance the journal entry if (1) a debit amount was entered for the first account selected and (2) the next account chosen normally has a credit balance.

➤ *Continue entering information for each account in the journal entry.*

G. Verify that the Amount in the Difference Box is Zero

Before the journal entry can be posted, debits must equal credits. If the entry is unbalanced, an amount other than zero appears in the Difference box in the bottom right corner of the window.

 Review the contents of the Difference box. If there is an amount in the box other than zero, the entry is unbalanced and you must correct the entry. If the amount in the Difference box is zero, go to step H.

H. Click the Show Button

 Click the Show button to reveal the account name (Description) boxes in the scrolling window.

I. Review the Transaction Entry Window for Completeness and Accuracy

Before the transaction is posted, most errors can be corrected by clicking the box with the error and making the correction. Certain boxes cannot be changed after they are originally completed. Errors in these boxes can only be corrected by deleting the journal entry and entering it again.

 Review the Transaction Entry window for completeness and accuracy. If you find an error while reviewing the window, click the box with the error and make corrections.

 If the box with the error cannot be accessed or changed, click the Delete button and click Delete again when asked if you are sure that you want to delete this transaction. Enter the transaction again by returning to step B.

J. Post the General Journal Entry

 After you are satisfied with all of the data in the Transaction Entry window, click the Post button to post the journal entry.

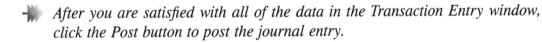

Journal Entry Review

Unlike other windows, the Transaction Entry window posts directly to the general ledger. To determine if the journal entry has been correctly posted, complete the following steps:

- *Click Financial → Detail (I) to open the Detail Inquiry window.*
- *Use the Account lookup button to select one of the accounts used in the journal entry just posted or type the account number.*
- *If the default year in the Year box is not correct, use the adjacent drop-down list to select the correct year or type the correct year.*
- *Locate the number of the journal entry just posted and click once on its line.*
- *Zoom on the Journal Entry description field to open the Transaction Entry Zoom window for the selected journal entry.*

The window that appears is a replica of the Transaction Entry window for the selected journal entry. It is not possible to change information through the Transaction Entry Zoom window. By clicking the Show button, you can review details for each account in the journal entry.

- *After reviewing the Transaction Entry Zoom window for the journal entry just posted, close the window and close the Detail Inquiry window.*

Error Correction After Posting a General Journal Entry

If you discover an error after posting a general journal entry, refer to Appendix A.

This page is intentionally blank.

Adjust Perpetual Inventory Records

Overview

The Item Transaction Entry window is used to process and record an adjustment of perpetual inventory records to equal the physical count. After an inventory adjustment is processed, the transaction updates the perpetual inventory records in *Microsoft Dynamics GP*. Later, when the transaction is posted to the general ledger, various accounts are affected depending upon the type of transaction. For example, if the physical quantity of inventory is less than the quantity in the perpetual records, cost of goods sold or an inventory shrinkage account is debited and inventory is credited.

Quick Reference Table

Step	Box or Other Location	Procedure
A	Navigation Pane buttons	Click *Inventory* ➔ *Transaction Entry (T)*.
B	Document Type	Select Variance as the document type.
C	Date	Review the default transaction date and change if necessary.
D	Default Site ID	Select the default site where the inventory is located.
E	Item Number	Select the item number of the inventory item being adjusted.
F	Quantity	Type the quantity adjustment for the selected inventory item (use a minus sign to reduce the perpetual quantity to match the physical count).
G	Unit Cost and Site ID boxes	Move through the Unit Cost and Site ID boxes.
H	Various	Repeat steps E through G for each type of inventory item being adjusted.
I	Item Transaction Entry window	Review the Item Transaction Entry window for completeness and accuracy.
J	Post button	Post the adjustment to the perpetual inventory records.

Adjust Perpetual Inventory Records
Dynamics Window

Item Transaction Entry Window
Inventory → Transaction Entry (T) **A**

I | **Item Transaction Entry**

File   Edit   Tools   View   He **J**   sa Jackson Supply Company 2/1/2010

💾 Save   ✖ Delete   📇 Post

Document Type: Variance **B**   Batch ID

Number   000001

Date   2/1/2010 **C** ⊞ →   Default Site ID **D**

Item Number **E**	U of M	Quantity **F**	Unit Cost **G**
Description			Site ID
		0	$0.00
			G
H			

Quantity Available   0.00   Distributions   Serial/Lot

|◀ ◀ ▶ ▶| Batch ID

Adjust Perpetual Inventory Records
Detailed Instructions

A. Click *Inventory* → *Transaction Entry (T)*

➤ *Click Inventory → Transaction Entry (T) to access the Item Transaction Entry window.*

B. Select Variance as the Document Type

➤ *Use the Document Type drop-down list to select Variance.*

C. Review the Default Transaction Date and Change if Necessary

➤ *If the date of the adjustment is different than the date shown, type the correct date.*

D. Select the Default Site where the Inventory is Located

➤ *Use the adjacent lookup button to select the default site where the inventory is located.*

E. Select the Item Number of the Inventory Item being Adjusted

➤ *Use the Item Number lookup button to select the inventory item being adjusted.*

F. Type the Quantity Adjustment for the Selected Inventory Item

The Quantity box is used to enter the increase or decrease adjustment for the selected inventory item. To reduce perpetual records to equal the physical quantity, a minus sign must precede the quantity. For example, if the perpetual records show a quantity of 25 and the physical count is 20, you must type [-5]. To increase the perpetual records to equal the physical quantity, only the quantity needs to be typed. For example, if the perpetual records show a quantity of 42 and the physical count is 46, you must type [4].

➤ *Type the quantity adjustment for the selected inventory item.*

G. Move Through the Unit Cost and Site ID Boxes

The Unit Cost and Site ID boxes are already filled with the correct default information. In order to enter the Item Number box for the next inventory item being adjusted, however, you need to move through these two boxes.

➤ *Press* [Return] *repeatedly until the cursor reaches the next blank Item Number box.*

H. Repeat Steps E through G for Each Type of Inventory Item being Adjusted

➤ *Continue entering information for each type of inventory item being adjusted.*

I. Review the Item Transaction Entry Window for Completeness and Accuracy

Before the transaction is posted, most errors can be corrected by choosing the box with the error and making the correction. Certain boxes cannot be changed after they are originally completed. Errors in these boxes can only be corrected by deleting the transaction and entering the transaction again.

➤ *Review the Item Transaction Entry window for completeness and accuracy. If you find an error while reviewing the window, click the box with the error and make corrections.*

➤ *If the box with the error cannot be accessed or changed, click the Delete button and click Delete again when asked if you are sure that you want to delete this transaction. Enter the transaction again by returning to step B.*

J. Post the Adjustment to the Perpetual Inventory Records

➤ *After you are satisfied with all of the data in the Item Transaction Entry window, click the Post button to post the transaction.*

Transaction Review

After clicking the Post button in the Item Transaction Entry window, you can determine if the transaction has been posted to the perpetual inventory records by completing the steps that follow. Recall that the transaction has not yet been posted to the general ledger.

- ➡ *Click Inventory* ➔ *Transaction (I) to open the Inventory Transaction Inquiry window.*
- ➡ *Select Variance as the document type.*
- ➡ *Use the Number lookup button to select the document number of the transaction you want to review.*
- ➡ *After reviewing the transaction, click the OK button or close the window.*

After an adjustment to the perpetual inventory records has been posted, you can also check the quantities on hand for the items that were adjusted by completing the following steps:

- ➡ *Click Inventory* ➔ *Item (C) to open the Item Maintenance window.*
- ➡ *Use the Item Number lookup button to select the first item adjusted.*
- ➡ *Review the amount in the Quantity on Hand box in the lower right corner. If the quantity is incorrect, take note of the quantity correction required before moving on to the next inventory item.*
- ➡ *Repeat the previous two steps for all remaining items.*
- ➡ *If there are quantity errors for any of the items, record another transaction to correct them.*

Error Correction After Posting a Transaction

If you discover an error after posting an adjustment to the perpetual inventory records, refer to Appendix A.

This page is intentionally blank.

Prepare a Bank Reconciliation

Overview

The Reconcile Bank Statements window is used to prepare periodic bank reconciliations. After a bank reconciliation is done, the checkbook register is updated for adjustments such as service charges, interest earned, unrecorded transactions, and errors. Later, when the adjustments are posted to the general ledger, the cash balance is adjusted. Other general ledger accounts that may be adjusted include interest income and bank service charge expense.

Quick Reference Table

Step	Box or Other Location	Procedure
A	Navigation Pane buttons	Click *Financial* → *Reconcile Bank Statement (T)*.
B	Checkbook ID	Select the checkbook ID of the bank account being reconciled.
C	Bank Statement Ending Balance	Type the bank statement ending balance.
D	Bank Statement Ending Date	Type the bank statement ending date.
E	Cutoff Date	Type the cutoff date for the bank reconciliation.
F	Transactions button	Click the Transactions button to access the Select Bank Transactions window.
G	"C" column check boxes (steps G-I are in the Select Bank Transactions window)	Click the "C" column check box next to each deposit and check transaction that cleared on the bank statement (or see step G on page 110 to select a range of numbers).
H	Difference	Review and analyze the contents of the Difference box.
I	Adjustments button	Click the Adjustments button to access the Reconcile Bank Adjustments window.
J	Show button (steps J-P are in the Reconcile Bank Adjustments window on page 108)	Click the Show button.
K	Type	Select the type of adjustment to be posted to the general ledger.
L	Date	Review the default adjustment date and change if necessary.
M	Account	Select or type the general ledger account number.
N	Checkbook Amount	Type the amount of the adjustment.
O	Various	Repeat steps K through N for each type of adjustment.
P	OK button	Click the OK button after all adjustments are entered.
Q	Difference box (steps Q & R are back in the Select Bank Transactions window)	Review the contents of the Difference box and resolve any remaining amount.
	Be sure to print your reconciliation reports [File → Print] before going on to the next step.	
R	Reconcile button	Click the Reconcile button.

Prepare a Bank Reconciliation
Dynamics Windows

Reconcile Bank Statements Window
Financial → Reconcile Bank Statement (T) **A**

Reconcile Bank Statements

File   Edit   Tools   View   Range   Help   2/15/2010 »

💾 Save | ✕ Delete

Checkbook ID   **B**
Description
Currency ID

Bank Statement Ending Balance   **C**
Bank Statement Ending Date   **D**
Cutoff Date   **E**   **F** Transactions

Select Bank Transactions Window

Select Bank Transactions

File   Edit   Tools   View   Range   Help   sa Fabrikam, Inc. 4/12/2017

Checkbook ID   UPTOWN TRUST   Display: All   Sort: by Type

Select Range ▾   Redisplay

		Type	Number	Date	C	Payment	→	Deposit	→
		DEP	20001	1/9/2014	☐	$0.00		$130,368.25	
		DEP	20002	1/16/2014	☐	$0.00		$228,576.73	
		DEP	20003	1/23/2014	☐	$0.00		$161,252.58	
		DEP	20004	1/23/2014	☐	$0.00		$460,357.76	
		DEP	20005	1/31/2014	☐	$0.00		$17,567.11	
		DEP	20006	1/31/2014	☐	$0.00		$16,956.84	
		DEP	20007	1/31/2014	☐	$0.00		$46,477.47	
		DEP	20008	1/31/2014	☐	$0.00		$100,939.66	
		CHK	1000.1	8/1/2013	☐	-$395.59		$0.00	
		CHK	1000.2	7/25/2013	☐	-$1,000.00		$0.00	
		CHK	1004.1	10/15/2013	☐	-$5,000.00		$0.00	

G

Cleared Transactions

	No. of	Total Amount		
Payments	0	$0.00		
Deposits	0	$0.00		

Adjusted Bank Balance	$574,099.26
Adjusted Book Balance	$575,075.98
Difference **H** **Q**	-$976.72 →

I Adjustments

OK   **R** Reconcile

Prepare a Bank Reconciliation
Dynamics Windows, continued

Reconcile Bank Adjustments Window

Reconcile Bank Adjustments				
File Edit Tools View Range Help			sa Fabrikam, Inc. 4/12/2017	

Checkbook ID	UPTOWN TRUST	Computer-Uptown Trust
Cash Account	000 -1100 -00	Cash - Operating Account

Cleared Difference	$0.00	Currency ID	Z-US$

Type	Date	→ Account	Checkbook Amount
Number	Description		Functional Amount
Distribution Reference			Currency ID
Interest Income **(K)**	1/31/20 **(L)**	- - **(M)**	**(N)** $0.00

(O)

(J)

Net Adjustment	$0.00
Reconcile Difference	-$976.72
Difference	$976.72

(P) OK

Prepare a Bank Reconciliation
Detailed Instructions

A. Click *Financial → Reconcile Bank Statement (T)*

> *Click Financial → Reconcile Bank Statement (T) to access the Reconcile Bank Statements window.*

B. Select the Checkbook ID of the Bank Account being Reconciled

> *Select the checkbook ID of the bank account being reconciled.*

C. Type the Bank Statement Ending Balance

> *Type the bank statement ending balance.*

D. Type the Bank Statement Ending Date

> *Type the bank statement ending date.*

E. Type the Cutoff Date for the Bank Reconciliation

The cutoff date is used by the software to determine which posted transactions and the ending recorded general ledger cash balance to include in the bank reconciliation process. All posted transactions on or before the selected cutoff date that have not been reconciled or voided will be included in the reconciliation. Most often, the cutoff date is the same as the ending date on the bank statement.

> *Type the cutoff date for the bank reconciliation.*

F. Click the Transactions Button to Access the Select Bank Transactions Window

The Transactions button in the bottom right corner of the window provides access to the second window used during the bank reconciliation process, the Select Bank Transactions window (see page 107 for illustration).

> *Click the Transactions button to open the Select Bank Transactions window.*

G. Click the "C" Column Box Next to each Deposit and Check Transaction that Cleared on the Bank Statement

The Select Bank Transactions window displays all posted transactions on or before the cutoff date that have not been reconciled or voided. The check boxes in the "C" column of the scrolling window of posted transactions are used to select which of the transactions cleared on the bank statement. When you first access the window, all boxes in the "C" column are unmarked. When you click a check box to select a transaction clearing on the bank statement, a check mark appears in the check box.

➡ *Click the "C" column check box next to each transaction that cleared on the bank statement.*

To select a range of transactions that cleared on the bank statement, complete the following steps:

➡ *Click the "C" column check box next to the first transaction in the range.*
➡ *Click Range (Menu Bar) → Begin Range.*
➡ *Click the "C" column check box next to the last transaction in the range.*
➡ *Click Range → End Range.*
➡ *Click Range → Mark.* This will mark each transaction in the selected range as cleared.

The above process can also be used to unmark a range of transactions, except click Unmark instead of Mark in the last step.

H. Review and Analyze the Contents of the Difference Box

After all cleared transactions are marked, there may still be an amount in the Difference box. The difference may result from any of the following three items (or a combination of the three items):

(1) Items clearing or not clearing the bank were not properly identified. Either the "C" column check box was not marked for an item that cleared the bank, or the "C" column check box was marked for an item that did not clear the bank.

(2) There is a bank error. The bank should be notified of the error, but no adjustment is needed to the general ledger.

(3) An adjustment needs to be recorded in the general ledger for service charges, interest income, and/or errors in the recording of checks or cash receipts in the general ledger.

 If situation (1) exists, return to step G and make the necessary corrections. When the Difference box contains zero, skip to step R.

 If situation (2) exists, contact the bank and obtain corrected bank statement information. Return to the Reconcile Bank Statements window and enter the corrected bank information. When the Difference box contains zero, skip to step R.

 If situation (3) exists, go to step I.

I. Click the Adjustments Button to Access the Reconcile Bank Adjustments Window

If there is a remaining difference to reconcile, you must access the Reconcile Bank Adjustments Window to record service charges, interest income, and other adjustments to the general ledger cash balance.

 Click the Adjustments button to access the Reconcile Bank Adjustments window.

J. Click the Show Button

 Click the Show button.

K. Select the Type of Adjustment to be Posted to the General Ledger

The following adjustment types are available: interest income, other income, other expense, and service charge.

➤ *Use the Type drop-down list to select the type of adjustment to be posted to the general ledger.*

L. Review the Default Adjustment Date and Change if Necessary

Microsoft Dynamics GP uses the bank statement ending date as the default date for the adjustment.

➤ *Press* [Return] *to accept the default date or type the correct date.*

M. Select or Type the General Ledger Account Number

Depending upon the type of adjustment selected in step K, the software either debits or credits the cash account being reconciled. The Account box is used to enter the offsetting account number for the adjustment entry. For example, an adjustment for interest income is posted as a credit to an interest income (revenue) account.

➤ *Use the Account lookup button to select the general ledger account number to offset the cash portion of the adjustment entry, or type the account number.*

N. Type the Amount of the Adjustment

➤ *Type the amount of the adjustment.*

O. Repeat Steps K through N for each Type of Adjustment

➤ *Continue entering information for each type of adjustment.*

P. Click the OK Button after all Adjustments are Entered

➤ *When all adjustments have been entered correctly, the amount in the Difference box of the Reconcile Bank Adjustments window is zero. Click the OK button to return to the Select Bank Transactions window.*

Q. Review the Contents of the Difference Box and Resolve any Remaining Amount

 If there is still an amount in the Difference box in the Select Bank Transactions window, return to step H to resolve the difference.

R. Click the Reconcile Button

Warning: After the Reconcile button is clicked, you cannot return to the bank reconciliation for that month to make corrections. If you need more time to locate and resolve your differences, you can click the OK button, return to the Reconcile Bank Statements window, and click the Save button to save the reconciliation in process. Later, you can return to the Reconcile Bank Statements window to complete the bank reconciliation.

 When all differences are accounted for, click the Reconcile button to process the bank reconciliation.

Bank Reconciliation Review

After completing the bank reconciliation, you can determine if the reconciliation has been included in the system by completing the steps that follow. Recall that the bank reconciliation adjustments, such as service charges and interest income, have not yet been posted to the general ledger.

 Click Financial → Checkbook Register (I) to open the Checkbook Register Inquiry window.

 Select the Checkbook ID for the reconciled bank account.

 Click the Show button.

In the scrolling window there is a description field called "Reconciled". All transactions listed in the scrolling window have either a "Yes" or a "No" in the Reconciled box. A "Yes" indicates a transaction that has been reconciled in the bank reconciliation process, such as a deposit clearing with the bank statement. A "No" indicates a transaction that has not been reconciled, such as an outstanding check.

➡️ *Review all transactions in the scrolling window to see if they contain the proper entry (Yes or No) in the Reconciled box.*

➡️ *Determine that any adjustments recorded during the bank reconciliation process have been recorded in the checkbook register.* All adjustments should appear in the scrolling window.

➡️ *Close all inquiry windows.*

Error Correction After Completing a Bank Reconciliation

As discussed earlier, after the Reconcile button is clicked, you cannot return to a completed bank reconciliation to make corrections. If all of the reconciliation is correct, but an incorrect general ledger account was entered for an adjustment in the Reconcile Bank Adjustments window, you can correct this error by recording a general journal entry. See pages 94-98.

This page is intentionally blank.

Perform Maintenance Activities

Overview

The purposes of maintenance are to (1) add, (2) change or (3) delete default information for the six windows identified on the facing page. Information that is changed through maintenance can be categorized into two types:

(1) Information that makes it easier to record transactions. An example is information in a lookup box to identify customers.

(2) Information that directly affects the amounts recorded in subsequent transactions. Examples include a change in the unit selling price of a product and a pay rate increase for an employee.

In addition to the maintenance tasks described above, other areas of *Microsoft Dynamics GP* involve maintenance. For example, setting up a new company in *Microsoft Dynamics GP* requires knowledge of most maintenance windows and tasks. Chapter 9 provides instructions and practice for setting up a new company.

Accessing a Maintenance Window. The second column in the table on page 117 shows the sequence of steps necessary to access each maintenance window. Notice that all selections for maintenance are from the Cards category.

Additional Windows within each Maintenance Window. Each of the six maintenance windows has additional windows (sub-windows) that are accessed from the main window. These sub-windows contain additional information related to the main maintenance window. Only certain additional windows are used in the project.

Instructions for Each Type of Maintenance Window. Instructions for using each of the six types of maintenance windows is explained in a section that follows. Each section contains window illustrations, along with reference tables for adding, changing, and deleting a record. The Quick Reference Table on the facing page identifies the Reference book page numbers for each type of maintenance.

Perform Maintenance Activities

Quick Reference Table

Maintenance Window Name	Steps Necessary to Access Maintenance Window	Functions Performed by Maintenance Window
Customer Maintenance (pages 118-121)	Click *Sales* → *Customer (C)*	Used to add a new customer, view and/or change data for a customer on file, or delete a former customer.
Vendor Maintenance (pages 122-125)	Click *Purchasing* → *Vendor (C)*	Used to add a new vendor, view and/or change data for a vendor on file, or delete a former vendor.
Account Maintenance (pages 126-128)	Click *Financial* → *Account (C)*	Used to add a new general ledger account, view and/or change data for an account on file, or delete an account no longer being used.
Employee Maintenance (pages 130-133)	Click *HR & Payroll* → *Employee (C)*	Used to add a new employee, view and/or change existing employee information, or delete a former employee.
Item Maintenance (pages 134-138)	Click *Inventory* → *Item (C)*	Used to add a new inventory item, view and/or change existing information, or delete an item no longer being purchased or sold.
Asset General Information (fixed asset maintenance— pages 140-144)	Click *Financial* → *General (C)* Note: General is under the Fixed Assets section of the Cards category.	Used to add a new fixed asset, view and/or change existing information, or retire an asset upon sale or other disposition.

Customer Maintenance

The following table includes instructions to add a customer record using the Customer Maintenance window shown at the top of page 119. For additional window illustrations, see the bottom of page 119 and page 120. *Note: See page 121 for instructions to change an existing customer's record or to delete a former customer's record.*

Instructions to Add a Customer Record

Location	Procedure
Navigation Pane buttons	Click *Sales* → *Customer (C)*.
Customer ID box (See Customer Maintenance window on top of page 119)	Type the customer ID.
Name box	Type the customer name.
Class ID box	Select the Class ID for the new customer.
Address ID box	Type [PRIMARY] in the Address ID box.
Customer Maintenance window	Complete the remaining boxes in the Customer Maintenance window on the top of the next page for the new customer, to the extent the information is available. Some boxes may be inapplicable to the new customer.
Customer Account Maintenance window (bottom of page 119)	Click the Accounts button to access the Customer Account Maintenance window. Review the default general ledger accounts for the new customer and change the information if necessary. Click the OK button.
Customer Maintenance Options window (page 120)	Click the Options button to access the Customer Maintenance Options window. Review the default information for the new customer and change the information if necessary. Click the OK button.
Customer Maintenance window	Review the contents of the Customer Maintenance window for completeness and accuracy.
Save button — Customer Maintenance window	Click the Save button to save the new customer record.

Customer Maintenance
Dynamics Windows

Customer Maintenance Window
Sales → Customer (C)

Customer Account Maintenance Window

Customer Maintenance
Dynamics Windows, continued

Customer Maintenance Options Window

Notes:

(1) The default information in each window will differ depending on the company and Class ID selected.

(2) The Customer Address Maintenance window will not be used in the project.

Customer Maintenance

The following tables include instructions to change information in an existing customer's record or to delete a former customer's record using the Customer Maintenance window. See pages 119 and 120 for window illustrations.

Instructions to Change Information in an Existing Customer's Record

Location	Procedure
Navigation Pane buttons	Click *Sales* ➔ *Customer (C)*.
Customer ID box (Customer Maintenance window)	Select the Customer ID of the customer whose record is to be changed.
Customer Maintenance, Customer Account Maintenance, and Customer Maintenance Options windows	Determine which customer maintenance window contains the information to be changed. Access the window if it is not already on the screen and enter the revised information.
Save button — Customer Maintenance window	Click the Save button to save the revised customer record.

Instructions to Delete a Former Customer's Record

Location	Procedure
Navigation Pane buttons	Click *Sales* ➔ *Customer (C)*.
Customer ID box (Customer Maintenance window)	Select the Customer ID of the customer being deleted.
Delete button	Click the Delete button to delete the customer.
Microsoft Dynamics GP's "delete this record" message	When the delete message appears, click Delete to delete the customer.
Second message	If there are transactions in the current year or a balance due from a prior year for the selected customer, a warning message appears saying that you cannot delete the customer's record. If the warning message appears, click the OK button.

Vendor Maintenance

The following table includes instructions to add a vendor record using the Vendor Maintenance window shown at the top of page 123. For additional window illustrations, see the bottom of page 123 and page 124. *Note: See page 125 for instructions to change an existing vendor's record or to delete a former vendor's record.*

Instructions to Add a Vendor Record

Location	Procedure
Navigation Pane buttons	Click *Purchasing* → *Vendor (C)*.
Vendor ID box (See Vendor Maintenance window on top of page 123)	Type the Vendor ID for the new vendor.
Name box	Type the vendor's name.
Class ID box	Select the Class ID for the new vendor.
Address ID box	Type [PRIMARY] in the Address ID box.
Vendor Maintenance window	Complete the remaining boxes in the Vendor Maintenance window on the top of the next page for the new vendor, to the extent the information is available. Some boxes may be inapplicable to the new vendor.
Vendor Maintenance Options window (bottom of page 123)	Click the Options button to access the Vendor Maintenance Options window. Review the default information for the new vendor and change the information if necessary. Click the OK button.
Vendor Account Maintenance window (page 124)	Click the Accounts button to access the Vendor Account Maintenance window. Review the default general ledger accounts for the new vendor and change the information if necessary. Click the OK button.
Vendor Maintenance window	Review the contents of the Vendor Maintenance window for completeness and accuracy.
Save button — Vendor Maintenance window	Click the Save button to save the new vendor record.

Vendor Maintenance
Dynamics Windows

Vendor Maintenance Window
Purchasing → *Vendor (C)*

Vendor Maintenance Options Window

Vendor Maintenance
Dynamics Windows, continued

Vendor Account Maintenance Window

Notes:

(1) The default information in each window will differ depending on the company and Class ID selected.

(2) The Vendor Address Maintenance window will not be used in the project.

Vendor Maintenance

The following tables include instructions to change information in an existing vendor's record or to delete a former vendor's record using the Vendor Maintenance window. See pages 123 and 124 for window illustrations.

Instructions to Change Information in an Existing Vendor's Record

Location	Procedure
Navigation Pane buttons	Click *Purchasing* → *Vendor (C)*.
Vendor ID box (Vendor Maintenance window)	Select the Vendor ID of the vendor whose record is to be changed.
Vendor Maintenance, Vendor Maintenance Options, and Vendor Account Maintenance windows	Determine which vendor maintenance window contains the information to be changed. Access the window if it is not already on the screen and enter the revised information.
Save button — Vendor Maintenance window	Click the Save button to save the revised vendor record.

Instructions to Delete a Former Vendor's Record

Location	Procedure
Navigation Pane buttons	Click *Purchasing* → *Vendor (C)*.
Vendor ID box (Vendor Maintenance window)	Select the Vendor ID of the vendor being deleted.
Delete button	Click the Delete button to delete the vendor.
Microsoft Dynamics GP's "delete this record" message	When the delete message appears, click Delete to delete the vendor.
Second message	If there are transactions in the current year or a balance due from a prior year for the selected vendor, a warning message appears saying that you cannot delete the vendor's record. If the warning message appears, click the OK button.

General Ledger Account Maintenance

The following table includes instructions to add a general ledger account record using the Account Maintenance window shown on page 127. *See page 128 for instructions to change an existing general ledger account's record or to delete a general ledger account record no longer being used.*

Instructions to Add a General Ledger Account Record

Location	Procedure
Navigation Pane buttons	Click *Financial → Account (C)*.
Account box (see Account Maintenance window on page 127)	Type the new general ledger account number.
Description box	Type the title of the new general ledger account.
Category box	Select the general ledger account category using the lookup button.
Posting Type radio buttons	Select the new account's posting type: Balance Sheet or Profit and Loss.
Typical Balance radio buttons	Select the new account's typical balance: Debit or Credit.
Account Maintenance window	Review the contents of the Account Maintenance window for completeness and accuracy.
Save button	Click the Save button to save the new general ledger account record.

General Ledger Account Maintenance
Dynamics Window

Account Maintenance Window
Financial ➔ *Account (C)*

Note: The Account Summary, Account History, Single-Account Budget Maintenance, and Select Account Currencies windows will not be used in the project.

General Ledger Account Maintenance

The following tables include instructions to change information in an existing general ledger account record or to delete a general ledger account record no longer being used. See page 127 for an illustration of the Account Maintenance window.

Instructions to Change Information in an Existing General Ledger Account's Record

Location	Procedure
Navigation Pane buttons	Click *Financial* → *Account (C)*.
Account box (Account Maintenance window)	Select the general ledger account to be changed.
Various	Determine which box contains the information to be changed. Enter the revised information.
Save button — Account Maintenance window	Click the Save button to save the revised general ledger account record.

Instructions to Delete a General Ledger Account Record No Longer Being Used

Location	Procedure
Navigation Pane buttons	Click *Financial* → *Account (C)*.
Account box (Account Maintenance window)	Select the general ledger account being deleted.
Delete button	Click the Delete button to delete the general ledger account.
Microsoft Dynamics GP's "delete this account" message	When the delete message appears, click Delete to delete the general ledger account.
Second message	If there are transactions in the current year or a balance carried forward from a prior year for the selected account, a warning message appears saying that you cannot delete the account. If the warning message appears, click the OK button.

This page is intentionally blank.

Employee Maintenance

The following table includes instructions to add an employee record using the Employee Maintenance window on the top of page 131. For additional window illustrations, see the bottom of page 131 and page 132. *Note: See page 133 for instructions to change an existing employee's record or to delete a former employee's record.*

Instructions to Add an Employee Record

Location	Procedure
Navigation Pane buttons	Click *HR & Payroll* ➔ *Employee (C)*.
Employee ID box (see Employee Maintenance window on top of page 131)	Type the Employee ID for the new employee.
Class ID box	Select the Class ID for the new employee. Click Yes when asked if you want to use default information from the class record. Another message appears mentioning the Human Resources module. Click Yes.
Address ID box	Type [PRIMARY] in the Address ID box.
Employee Maintenance window	Complete the remaining boxes in the Employee Maintenance window on the top of the next page for the new employee, to the extent the information is available. Some boxes may be inapplicable.
Employee Additional Information Maintenance window (bottom of page 131)	Click the Additional Information button to access the Employee Additional Information Maintenance window. Type the employee's birth date in the Birth Date box. Click the OK button and close the window.
Employee Maintenance window	Click the Save button. A message appears asking if you want to save the changes to History. Click No.
Employee Pay Code Maintenance window (top of page 132)	Select the Employee ID of the employee you just added. Click the Go To button in the top right corner of the Employee Maintenance window. Click the Payroll option, then click the Pay Codes menu selection to access the Employee Pay Code Maintenance window. **For salaried employees:** (1) Use the Pay Code lookup button to select the pay code for salaried employees. (2) Type the employee's pay rate in the Pay Rate box (amount of salary per pay period). (3) Click the Save button. (4) Click "No" when asked if you want to roll down the change to other pay codes. Close the Employee Pay Code Maintenance window. **For hourly employees:** (1) Use the Pay Code lookup button to select the pay code for regular hourly pay. (2) Type the employee's regular hourly pay rate in the Pay rate box. (3) Click the Save button. (4) If the employee's overtime pay rate is based on a factor of his or her hourly pay rate, click "Yes" when asked if you want to roll down the change to other pay codes. Otherwise, click "No." (5) If the employee also has an overtime pay rate, use the Pay Code lookup button to select the pay code for overtime pay. (6) If the employee's overtime pay rate is based on a factor of his or her hourly pay rate, enter the factor in the Pay Factor box (enter 1.5 for example). If the employee's overtime pay rate is not based on a factor of his or her hourly pay rate, type the overtime pay rate in the Pay Rate box. (7) Click the Save button. Close the Employee Pay Code Maintenance window.
Employee Tax Maintenance window (bottom of page 132)	Click the Go To button in the top right corner of the Employee Maintenance window. Click the Payroll option, then click the Tax Information menu selection to access the Employee Tax Maintenance window. Complete the remaining portions of the window, to the extent the information is applicable and available. Click the Save button. Close the window.
Employee Maintenance window	Review the contents of the Employee Maintenance window for completeness and accuracy.
Save button — Employee Maintenance window	Click the Save button to save the new employee record.

Employee Maintenance
Dynamics Windows

Employee Maintenance Window
HR & Payroll → *Employee (C)*

Employee Additional Information Maintenance Window

Employee Maintenance
Dynamics Windows, continued

Employee Pay Code Maintenance Window

Employee Tax Maintenance Window

Notes:

(1) The default information in each window will differ depending on the company and Class ID selected.

(2) The Employee Address Maintenance and the Employee Vacation-Sick Time Maintenance windows will not be used in this project.

Employee Maintenance

The following tables include instructions to change information in an existing employee's record or to delete a former employee's record using the Employee Maintenance window. See pages 131 and 132 for window illustrations.

Instructions to Change Information in an Existing Employee's Record

Location	Procedure
Navigation Pane buttons	Click *HR & Payroll* → *Employee (C)* (or other appropriate window option).
Employee ID box (Employee Maintenance window)	Select the Employee ID of the employee whose record is to be changed.
Employee Maintenance, Employee Additional Information Maintenance, Employee Pay Code Maintenance, and Employee Tax Maintenance windows	Determine which employee maintenance window contains the information to be changed. Use the Additional Information button or the Go To button to access the appropriate window if it is not already on the screen and enter the revised information. Click *HR & Payroll* → *Pay Code (C)* for a change of pay rates, and identify salary, hourly, and overtime by first selecting the Pay Code, then changing the rate of pay. Click the Save button after each Pay Code change. For hourly employees whose overtime pay rate is based on a factor of their regular pay rate, click "Yes" to roll down the hourly pay code change to other pay codes. Otherwise, click "No."
Save button — Employee Maintenance window	Click the Save button to save the revised employee record. When asked for a reason for the change, select the reason and click OK.

Instructions to Delete a Former Employee's Record

Location	Procedure
Navigation Pane buttons	Click *HR & Payroll* → *Employee (C)*.
Employee ID box (Employee Maintenance window)	Select the Employee ID of the employee being deleted.
Delete button	Click the Delete button to delete the employee.
Microsoft Dynamics GP's "delete this record" message	When the delete message appears, click Delete to delete the employee.
Second message	If there are transactions in the current year for the selected employee, a warning message appears saying that you cannot delete the employee's record. If the warning message appears, click the OK button.

Inventory Item Maintenance

The following table includes instructions to add an inventory item record using the Item Maintenance window shown at the top of page 135. For additional window illustrations, see the bottom of page 135 and pages 136-137. *Note: See page 138 for instructions to change an inventory item's record or to delete an inventory item no longer being purchased or sold.*

Instructions to Add an Inventory Item Record

Location	Procedure
Navigation Pane buttons	Click *Inventory* ➔ *Item (C)*.
Class ID box (see Item Maintenance window on top of page 135)	Select the Class ID for the new inventory item. Click Yes when asked if you want to update the item with default information from the selected class.
Item Maintenance window (top of page 135)	Complete the remaining boxes in the Item Maintenance window, to the extent the information is available. Some boxes may be inapplicable.
Item Account Maintenance window (bottom of page 135)	Click the Accounts button to access the Item Account Maintenance window. Review the default general ledger accounts and change the information if necessary. Click the OK button.
Item Price List Maintenance window (top of page 136)	Click the Go To button in the top right corner of the Item Maintenance window. Click the Price List menu option to access the Item Price List Maintenance window. Click Yes when asked if you want to save the changes first. Next, copy the price level information from an existing inventory item to the new item. To do this, click the Copy button. Use the Source Item Number lookup button to select any inventory item already on file. Click the Process button. Click the Cancel button in the Report Destination window. Click the Save button to save the price list information and then close the Item Price List Maintenance window.
Item Quantities Maintenance window (bottom of page 136)	Click the Go To button in the top right corner of the Item Maintenance window. Click the Quantities/Sites menu option to access the Item Quantities Maintenance window. Click the Site ID radio button. Use the Site ID lookup button to select the site where the inventory will be held. Click the Save button. Click the All radio button next to the Sites description field. Use the Default Site ID lookup button to select the site to be used as the default site for purchases. Click Save and close the window.
Item Purchasing Options Maintenance window (top of page 137)	Click the Go To button in the top right corner of the Item Maintenance window. Click the Purchasing menu option to access the Item Purchasing Options Maintenance window. Select the default purchasing unit of measure. Click Save and close the window.
Item Vendors Maintenance window (bottom of page 137)	Click the Go To button in the top right corner of the Item Maintenance window. Click the Vendors menu option to access the Item Vendors Maintenance window. Use the Vendor ID lookup button to select the vendor from whom the inventory is purchased. Type the vendor item number in the Vendor Item box (the default is the item number you entered in the main window). Click the Save button. Close the window.
Item Maintenance window	Review the contents of the Item Maintenance window for completeness and accuracy.
Save button — Item Maintenance window	Click the Save button to save the new inventory item record.

Inventory Item Maintenance
Dynamics Windows

Item Maintenance Window
Inventory → Item (C)

Item Maintenance				sa Jackson Supply Company 2/1/2010

File Edit Tools Additional Help

Save   Clear   ✕ Delete   Copy

Item Number			🔍 📄	
Description				ℹ
Short Description				
Generic Description			Class ID	🔍

Item Type:	Sales Inventory		Quantity Decimals:	0
Valuation Method:	FIFO Perpetual		Currency Decimals:	2

Sales Tax Option:	Taxable		Purchase Tax Option:	Taxable
Tax Schedule ID		🔍	Tax Schedule ID	🔍
U of M Schedule ID		🔍	Standard Cost	$0.00
			Current Cost	$0.00
Shipping Weight			List Price	$0.00

	Quantity On Hand	0
Options Accounts	Quantity Available	0

⏮ ◀ ▶ ⏭   by Item Number

Item Account Maintenance Window

Item Account Maintenance		sa Jackson Supply Company 2/1/2010

File Edit Tools Additional Help

Item Number	101
Description	Bath towels - 100 pack

	Account	Description	
Inventory	10400	🔍 Inventory	→
Inventory Offset	30400	🔍 Cost of Goods Sold	→
Cost of Goods Sold	30400	🔍 Cost of Goods Sold	→
Sales	30100	🔍 Sales	→
Markdowns	30100	🔍 Sales	→
Sales Returns	30200	🔍 Sales Returns	→
In Use	30400	🔍 Cost of Goods Sold	→
In Service	30400	🔍 Cost of Goods Sold	→
Damaged	30400	🔍 Cost of Goods Sold	→
Variance	30400	🔍 Cost of Goods Sold	→
Drop Ship Items	30400	🔍 Cost of Goods Sold	→
Purchase Price Variance		🔍	→
Unrealized Purch Price Var		🔍	→
Inventory Returns	10400	🔍 Inventory	→
Assembly Variance		🔍	→

OK

Inventory Item Maintenance
Dynamics Windows, continued

Item Price List Maintenance Window

Item Quantities Maintenance Window

Inventory Item Maintenance
Dynamics Windows, continued

Item Purchasing Options Maintenance Window

Item Vendors Maintenance Window

Notes:

(1) The default information in each window will differ depending on the company and Class ID selected.

(2) The following inventory maintenance windows will not be used in the project: Item Maintenance Options, Item Kit Maintenance, and Item History.

Inventory Item Maintenance

The following tables include instructions to change information in an inventory item's record or to delete an inventory item record no longer being purchased or sold using the Item Maintenance window. See pages 135-137 for window illustrations.

Instructions to Change Information in an Existing Inventory Item's Record

Location	Procedure
Navigation Pane buttons	Click *Inventory* ➔ *Item (C)*.
Item Number box (Item Maintenance window)	Select the Item Number of the inventory item record being changed.
Item Maintenance, Item Account Maintenance, Item Quantities Maintenance, and Item Vendors Maintenance windows	Determine which inventory maintenance window contains the information to be changed. Access the window if it is not already on the screen and enter the revised information.
Save button — Item Maintenance window	Click the Save button to save the revised inventory item record.

Instructions to Delete an Inventory Item No Longer being Purchased or Sold

Location	Procedure
Navigation Pane buttons	Click *Inventory* ➔ *Item (C)*.
Item Number box (Item Maintenance window)	Select the Item Number of the inventory item being deleted.
Quantity Available button	Look in the Quantity Available box. If the quantity is zero, skip to the next step. If there is a quantity greater than zero in this box, you cannot delete the item. Close Item Maintenance window.
Delete button	Click the Delete button to delete the inventory item record.
Microsoft Dynamics GP's "delete this record" message	When the delete message appears, click Delete to delete the inventory item record.
Second message	If there are transactions in the current year for the selected inventory item, a warning message appears saying that you cannot delete the record. If the warning message appears, click the OK button.

This page is intentionally blank.

Fixed Asset Maintenance

The following table includes instructions to add a fixed asset record using the Asset General Information window shown at the top of page 141. For additional window illustrations, see the bottom of page 141 and page 142. *Note: See page 143 for instructions to change a fixed asset record and page 144 for instructions to retire a fixed asset when it is sold.*

Instructions to Add a Fixed Asset Record

Note: For the purchase of a fixed asset, it must first be recorded through the appropriate transaction window (purchase on account—pages 60-66; purchase with a note—pages 94-98)

Location	Procedure
Navigation Pane buttons	Click *Financial* → *General (C)*.
Asset ID box (see Asset General Information window on the top of page 141)	Type an asset identification number in the Asset ID box. An example of an asset identification number is "000005."
Description box	Type a description of the new asset.
Class ID box	Select the Class ID for the new fixed asset. Class ID's are usually already set up for different types of assets such as vehicles, machinery and equipment, buildings, etc.
Acquisition Date box	Type the date the asset was acquired in the Acquisition Date box.
Acquisition Cost box	Type the cost of the asset in the Acquisition Cost box.
Date Added box	Type the date the asset was acquired in the Date Added box.
Save button	Click the Save button.
Asset Account window (bottom of page 141)	Click the Go To button in the top right corner of the Asset General Information window. Select the "Account" menu option to open the Asset Account window. Review the default posting accounts and make any necessary changes. Click the Save button. Close the Asset Account window.
Asset Book window (top of page 142)	Click the Go To button in the top right corner of the Asset General Information window. Select the "Book" menu option to open the Asset Book window. In the Book ID box, select the method that is used for corporate (book) reporting.* Review the information in the window. You will rarely need to modify the information in this window because most of it is determined by information entered in previous windows. Click the Save button and close the window.
Asset General Information window	Review the contents of the Asset General Information window for completeness and accuracy.
Save button — Asset General Information window	Click the Save button to save the new fixed asset record.

* The Book ID box is used to enter different methods of depreciation for the same asset for book depreciation, tax depreciation, and alternative minimum tax (AMT) depreciation. Only book depreciation is covered in this project.

Fixed Asset Maintenance
Dynamics Windows

Asset General Information Window
Financial → General (C)

```
┌─────────────────────────────────────────────────────────────────────┐
│ ▣ Asset General Information                              _ ▢ ✕      │
├─────────────────────────────────────────────────────────────────────┤
│  File   Edit   Tools   Help              sa  Jackson Supply Company 2/1/2010 │
│  💾 Save   ✐ Clear                              ☑ Redisplay    ▭▾   │
│                                                                       │
│  Asset ID          [          ▾ 🔍 ▯]        Status  [Active    ]    │
│  Description       [                      ]                           │
│  Extended Description [                   ]                           │
│  Short Name        [          ]                                       │
│  Master Asset ID   [        🔍]                                       │
│                                                                       │
│  Class ID          [        🔍]    Acquisition Date [        ▦]      │
│  Type:             [        ▾]      Currency ID     [           ]    │
│  Property Type:    [        ▾]      Acquisition Cost [          ]    │
│  Account Group ID  [        🔍]                                      │
│                                                                       │
│  Physical Loc ID   [       🔍→]    Location ID     [      🔍→]       │
│  Asset Label       [          ]                                       │
│  Structure ID      [        🔍]    Quantity        [      →]         │
│  Custodian         [        🔍]    Last Maintenance [   ▦ →]         │
│  Manufacturer Name [        →]     Date Added       [   ▦ →]         │
│                                                                       │
│  ☑ Auto Add Book Info                                                │
│  ◄◄ ◄ ► ►│  by Asset ID    ▾                              ▱ ⊙       │
└─────────────────────────────────────────────────────────────────────┘
```

Asset Account Window

```
┌─────────────────────────────────────────────────────────────────────┐
│ ▣ Asset Account                                          _ ▢ ✕      │
├─────────────────────────────────────────────────────────────────────┤
│  File   Edit   Tools   Help              sa  Jackson Supply Company 2/1/2010 │
│  💾 Save   ✐ Clear   ✕ Delete                   ☑ Redisplay    ▭▾   │
│                                                                       │
│  Asset ID     [00003]  [1   ▾ 🔍 ▯]     Status   [Active      ]      │
│                                                                       │
│  Account Group ID  [                    🔍]                          │
│                                                                       │
│  Accounts:                          Account Descriptions:            │
│  Depr. Expense      40400      🔍  Depreciation                      │
│  Depr. Reserve      10900      🔍  Accumulated Depreciation          │
│  Prior Year Depr.   40400      🔍  Depreciation                      │
│  Asset Cost         10800      🔍  Fixed Assets                      │
│  Proceeds           10810      🔍  Fixed Assets Clearing Account     │
│  Rec. Gain/Loss     30900      🔍  Gain/Loss on Sale of Fixed Assets │
│  Non Rec. Gain/Loss 30900      🔍  Gain/Loss on Sale of Fixed Assets │
│  Clearing           10810      🔍  Fixed Assets Clearing Account     │
│                                                                       │
│  ◄◄ ◄ ► ►│  by Asset ID    ▾                              ▱ ⊙       │
└─────────────────────────────────────────────────────────────────────┘
```

Fixed Asset Maintenance
Dynamics Windows, continued

Asset Book Window

```
Asset Book                                              [_][□][X]

 File   Edit   Tools   Help            sa  Jackson Supply Company  2/1/2010

 [💾] Save   [✎] Clear   [✕] Delete              [✓] Redisplay        [▭]▾

 Asset ID            00003        1    ▾ [Q][📄] Vehicles
 Book ID:                              ▾ [Q]
                                              Fully Depreciated Flag      [ ]
 Place in Service Date          [▦] →         Status:                [Active      ]
 Depreciated to Date            [▦]
 Begin Year Cost                     →        Original Life Year, Days  [00][000]
 Cost Basis                                   Remaining Year, Days      [00][000]
 Salvage Value
 Yearly Depr. Rate                   →
 Current Depreciation                →        Amortization Code:            [▾]
 YTD Depreciation                             Amortization Amt / Pct:
 LTD Depreciation                             Initial Allowance Pct          →
 Net Book Value                               Special Depr Allowance    [▾]      [÷]

 Depreciation Method:            [▾]          Luxury Automobile:     [▾]
 Averaging Convention:           [▾]          [ ] Luxury Van or Truck
 Switchover:                     [▾] →        [ ] Luxury Electric Auto

 [|◄][◄][►][►|]  by Asset ID      [▾]                          [📖] [?]
```

Retirement Maintenance Window

```
Retirement Maintenance                                  [_][□][X]

 File   Edit   Tools   Help            sa  Jackson Supply Company  2/1/2010

 [🧠] Retire   [✎] Clear   [✖] Cancel

 Asset ID              [          ] ▾ [Q][📄]
 Retirement Date       [        ][▦]              Retirement Event  [          ]
 Retirement Type       [          ] ▾
 Retirement Code       [        ] [Q]    Currency ID    [              ][ ][📄][÷]

 Quantity | Cost      | Percent | Cash Proceeds  | Non-Cash Proceeds | Expenses of Sale
                                  Originating Amounts                                 ▲
                                                                                      ▦
                                                                                      ▼

        0 |    $0.00  |  0.00%  |

 [|◄][◄][►][►|]  by Asset ID      [▾]                          [📖] [?]
```

Fixed Asset Maintenance

The following table includes instructions to change information in a fixed asset record. See page 141 and the top of page 142 for window illustrations. *For instructions to retire a fixed asset when it is sold, see page 144.*

Instructions to Change Information in an Existing Fixed Asset Record

Location	Procedure
Navigation Pane buttons	Click *Financial* ➔ *General (C)*.
Asset ID box (Asset General Information window)	Select the Asset ID of the fixed asset record to be changed.
Asset General Information, Asset Account, and Asset Book windows	Determine which fixed asset maintenance window contains the information to be changed. Access the window if it is not already on the screen, enter the revised information and click the Save button. ***Warning: Changes made in most boxes of the Asset General Information and Asset Book windows will affect depreciation calculations for the underlying asset. Do not make any depreciation-sensitive changes for this project.***

Fixed Asset Maintenance

The following table includes instructions to retire a fixed asset when it is sold. *See the bottom of page 142 for an illustration of the Retirement Maintenance window.*

Instructions to Retire a Fixed Asset When it is Sold

Location	Procedure
Navigation Pane buttons	Click *Financial* ➔ *Retire (T)*.*
Asset ID box (Retirement Maintenance window)	Use the Asset ID lookup button to select the asset being sold.
Retirement Date box	Type the sale date in the Retirement Date box.
Retirement Type box	Select Sale in the Retirement Type box.
Cost box	Type the cost basis of the asset being sold in the Cost box. For partial sales, type only the cost basis of the portion of the assets being sold.
Percent box	Do not change the contents of the Percent box. *Microsoft Dynamics GP* automatically calculates this box.
Cash Proceeds box or Non-Cash Proceeds box	For proceeds received in the form of cash or a check, type the net proceeds in the Cash Proceeds box. For noncash sales, type the net proceeds in the Non-Cash Proceeds box.**
Retire button	Click the Retire button. A message appears asking if you want to continue. Click OK. Another message appears saying that retirement is completed. Click OK. Close the Retirement Maintenance window.
Bank Transaction Entry window, Bank Deposit Entry window	*If you entered cash proceeds for the fixed asset sale,* refer to pages 42-46 to record a miscellaneous cash receipt. The amount of the net proceeds should be recorded as a debit to cash and a credit to the fixed assets clearing account. After recording the miscellaneous cash receipt, refer to pages 48-51 to record a bank deposit for the net proceeds.
Transaction Entry window	*If you entered noncash proceeds for the fixed asset sale,* refer to pages 94-98 to record a general journal entry. The amount of the net proceeds should be recorded as a debit to the account where the noncash proceeds belong (miscellaneous receivable, for example) and a credit to the fixed assets clearing account.

*   This is the only maintenance task that uses the Transactions category, not the Cards category.

** Net proceeds equal the gross selling price less expenses of sale. The Expenses of Sale box is not used in this project.

This page is intentionally blank.

Depreciate Fixed Assets and
Perform Other Annual Fixed Asset Procedures

Overview

Annual depreciation of fixed assets and related activities for fixed assets are done using three windows. *Microsoft Dynamics GP* does all depreciation calculations based on information previously entered through maintenance. After the process for all three windows is done, the fixed assets subsidiary records are updated. A batch entry is also prepared for later posting to the general ledger, which will update the following accounts: fixed assets, depreciation expense, accumulated depreciation, and gain or loss on the sale of fixed assets.

Quick Reference Table

Step	Box or Other Location	Procedure
A	Navigation Pane buttons	Click *Financial* → *Depreciate (RO)*.
B	Depreciation Target Date	Type the fiscal year-end date.
C	Books on file list box	Click the name that corresponds to the book method of depreciation.
D	Insert button	Click the Insert button.
E	Depreciate button	Click the Depreciate button.
F	All Assets message (not shown)	Click OK when the message appears asking if you want to depreciate all assets.
G	Close button	Close the Depreciation Process Information window.
H	Navigation Pane buttons	Click *Financial* → *GL Posting (RO)*. Note: this is in the Fixed Assets section of Routines.
I	Beginning Period	Type the beginning period of the fiscal year, using four digits for the year and three digits for the month.
J	Ending Period	Type the ending period of the fiscal year, using four digits for the year and three digits for the month.
K	Transaction Date	Type the date of the last day of the fiscal year.
L	Continue button	Click the Continue button.
M	Batch number message (not shown)	Click Continue when the batch number message appears.
N	Cancel button - Report Dest. window (not shown)	Click Cancel to close the Report Destination window.
O	Close button	Close the Fixed Asset General Ledger Posting window.
P	Navigation Pane buttons	Click *Financial* → *Year End (RO)*. Note: this is in the Fixed Assets section of Routines.
Q	Available Books list box	Click the name that corresponds to the current year's book method of depreciation.
R	Insert button	Click the Insert button.
S	Continue button	Click the Continue button.
T	Year-end processing message (not shown)	Click Continue when the year-end processing message appears.

Depreciate Fixed Assets and
Perform Other Annual Fixed Asset Procedures
Dynamics Windows

Depreciation Process Information Window
Financial → Depreciate (RO) Ⓐ

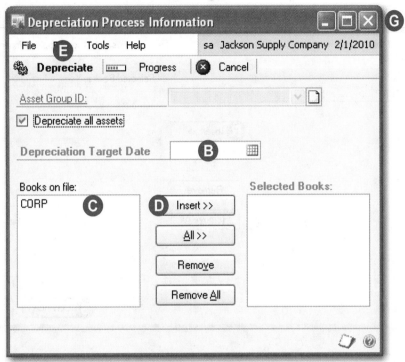

Asset General Ledger Posting Window
Financial → GL Posting (RO) Ⓗ

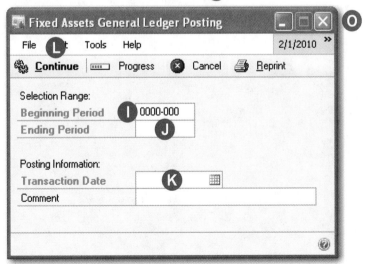

Depreciate Fixed Assets and
Perform Other Annual Fixed Asset Procedures
Dynamics Windows, continued

Asset Year End Window
Financial → Year End (RO) **P**

Depreciate Fixed Assets and
Perform Other Annual Fixed Asset Procedures
Detailed Instructions

A. Click *Financial → Depreciate (RO)*

> *Click Financial → Depreciate (RO) to access the Depreciation Process Information window.*

B. Type the Fiscal Year-end Date

> *Type the fiscal year-end date in the Depreciation Target Date box.*

C. Click the Name that Corresponds to the Book Method of Depreciation

> *Microsoft Dynamics GP* has the capability of calculating depreciation for book (financial statement), tax, and alternative minimum tax purposes. For simplicity, only book depreciation is covered in this project.

> *Click the name that corresponds to the book depreciation method in the Books on file list box to highlight the name.*

D. Click the Insert Button

> *Click the Insert button to insert the name of the book depreciation method into the Selected Books list box.*

E. Click the Depreciate Button

> *Click the Depreciate button to calculate depreciation for all assets.*

F. Click OK When the Message Appears Asking if You Want to Depreciate All Assets

> After completing step E, a message appears asking if you want to depreciate all assets.

> *Click OK when the message appears.*

G. Close the Depreciation Process Information Window

➡ *Click the close button to close the Depreciation Process Information window.*

H. Click *Financial → GL Posting (RO)*

The next step in the annual fixed assets procedures is to prepare a batch entry for all fixed assets activity for the fiscal year. The entry includes the depreciation calculations completed in steps A-G, as well as all additions and retirements of fixed assets. The batch entry is posted to the general ledger later when all other entries are also posted to the general ledger (see pages 154-157).

➡ *Click Financial → GL Posting (RO) to access the Fixed Asset General Ledger Posting window.*

I. Type the Beginning Period of the Fiscal Year, Using Four Digits for the and Three Digits for the Month

➡ *Type the beginning period of the fiscal year. For the year, type four digits (2009, for example). For the first month of the year, type three digits (001, for example).*

J. Type the Ending Period of the Fiscal Year, Using Four Digits for the Year and Three Digits for the Month

➡ *Type the ending period of the fiscal year. For the year, type four digits (2009, for example). For the last month of the year, type three digits (012, for example).*

K. Type the Date of the Last Day of the Fiscal Year

➡ *Type the date of the last day of the fiscal year in the Transaction Date box (123109, for example).*

L. Click the Continue Button

➡ *Click the Continue button to begin the depreciation calculations.*

M. Click Continue When the Batch Number Message Appears

After the Continue button is clicked in step L, a message appears saying that a batch number is being created and asking if you want to continue.

 Click Continue when the batch number message appears.

N. Click Cancel to Close the Report Destination Window

After the depreciation calculations are done, a Report Destination window appears on the screen. You do not need to review this report.

 Click Cancel to Close the Report Destination window.

O. Close the Fixed Asset General Ledger Posting Window

 Use the Close button to close the Fixed Asset General Ledger Posting window.

P. Click *Financial → Year End (RO)*

The next step in the fixed asset annual procedures is to close the current fiscal year for the fixed asset subsidiary records and prepare the records for the next year.

 Click Financial → Year End (RO) to access the Asset Year End window. Note: Be sure to select this from the Fixed Assets section of Routines, not the Financial section.

Q. Click the Name that Corresponds to the Current Year's Book Method of Depreciation

The Available Books list box contains a list of all depreciation methods for the company. As described earlier, *Microsoft Dynamics GP* has the capability to calculate depreciation for book, tax, and alternative minimum tax purposes. For this project, locate the current year's book method of depreciation in the Available Books list box.

 Review the list of depreciation books in the Available Books list box. Locate the current year's book depreciation and click once on its name to highlight it.

R. Click the Insert Button

➤ *Click the Insert button to insert the current year's book method of depreciation into the Selected Books list box.*

S. Click the Continue Button

➤ *Click the Continue button to begin the year-end closing process for fixed assets.*

T. Click Continue When the Year-end Processing Message Appears

After the Continue button is clicked in step S, a message appears stating that the year-end processing for fixed assets will be started.

➤ *To complete the year-end closing process for fixed assets and prepare the subsidiary records for the next fiscal year, click Continue when the year-end processing message appears.*

Depreciation Review

After depreciating all fixed assets, you can determine if the calculations are correct by completing the steps that follow. Recall that the depreciation and other fixed asset entries for additions and deletions have not yet been posted to the general ledger.

➤ *Click Financial → Book (I) to access the Asset Book Inquiry window.*
➤ *Select the Asset ID for the fixed asset record you want to review.*
➤ *Select the Book ID for the book method of depreciation.*
➤ *Review the amount in the Current Run Depr. box. If there is an error, refer to Appendix A.*
➤ *Select the Asset ID for the next fixed asset record you want to review. Review the amount in the Current Run Depr. box. Repeat this step for all other fixed assets. If there are errors, refer to Appendix A.*

Error Correction After Performing Annual Fixed Asset Procedures

If you discover an error after depreciating fixed assets for the fiscal year or after performing other annual fixed asset procedures, refer to Appendix A.

This page is intentionally blank.

Post Transactions to the General Ledger

Overview

To provide proper segregation of duties, many companies have different individuals responsible for accounts receivable, accounts payable, payroll, inventory, fixed assets, and the general ledger. Most accounting software packages, including *Microsoft Dynamics GP*, have separate modules for each of these areas.

Because the general ledger in *Microsoft Dynamics GP* is a separate module, the program posts transactions in a two-step process. First, posted transaction entry windows update subsidiary records such as customer records, vendor records, and perpetual inventory records. Next, groups of transactions are posted to the general ledger through the Series Posting window. Posting to the general ledger through the Series Posting window is discussed in this section.

Quick Reference Table

Step	Box or Other Location	Procedure
A	Navigation Pane buttons	Click *Financial* → *Series Post (T)*.
B	Mark All	Click the Mark All button.
C	Post	Click the Post button.

Post Transactions to the General Ledger
Dynamics Window

Series Posting Window
Financial → *Series Post (T)* **A**

Post Transactions to the General Ledger
Detailed Instructions

A. Click *Financial* → *Series Post (T)*

➤ *Click Financial → Series Post (T) to open the Series Posting window.*

B. Click the Mark All Button

When the Series Posting window opens, a listing of all transactions that have not been posted to the general ledger appears in the scrolling window. *Microsoft Dynamics GP* allows you to either select individual transaction lines for posting or select all unposted transactions using the Mark All button. The Mark All button is used for this project.

➤ *Click the Mark All button. After clicking the Mark All button, the Available check box next to each transaction should be checked. If it is not, click the Mark All button again.*

C. Click the Post Button

➤ *Click the Post button to post all transactions to the general ledger. As each transaction posts, it disappears from the scrolling window.*

Posting Review

After clicking the Post button in the Series Posting window, you can determine if a specific transaction has been posted to the general ledger by completing the steps that follow.

➤ *Click Financial → Detail (I).*

➤ *Use the Account lookup button to select one of the posting accounts for the selected transaction or type the account number.*

➤ *If the default year in the Year box is not correct, use the adjacent drop-down list to select the correct year or type the correct year.*

➤ *Locate the transaction in the scrolling window and click once on its line.*

➤ *Zoom on the Journal Entry description field to open the Transaction Entry Zoom window for the selected transaction.*

The window that appears shows the general journal entry posted to the general ledger when the transaction was posted through the Series Posting window. It is not possible to change information through the Transaction Entry Zoom window. For all transactions except general journal entries, you can zoom to the original transaction entry window by doing the following:

➤ *Zoom on the Source Document description field to open an inquiry window for the originating transaction.* Although you can review the originating transaction through the inquiry window, you cannot edit or delete it.

➤ *Close all inquiry windows.*

Age Accounts Receivable and
Print Customer Monthly Statements

Overview

Most companies prepare monthly statements of outstanding accounts receivable from customers. Before customer monthly statements can be prepared in *Microsoft Dynamics GP*, you must perform the aging routine for accounts receivable as of the end of the month. This process sorts accounts receivable into various aging categories, such as current, 1-30 days, 31-60 days, etc. The Receivables Aging Process window is used to complete the aging of accounts receivable. After outstanding accounts receivable are aged into the proper categories, you can print customer monthly statements using the Print Receivables Statements window.

Note: The Quick Reference Table below assumes that you do not want to print an aging schedule using this window. An aging schedule is prepared later. Also, the table assumes that you want to print only one customer statement.

Quick Reference Table

Step	Box or Other Location	Procedure
A	Navigation Pane buttons	Click *Sales* → *Aging (RO)*.
B	Aging Date	Review the aging date and change if necessary.
C	Continue button (not shown)	If you receive a message about time between aging date and user date, click the Continue button.
D	Process	Click the Process button.
E	Cancel button (Report Destination window, not shown)	Click the Cancel button in the Report Destination window.
F	Navigation Pane buttons	Click *Sales* → *Statements (RO)*.
G	Statement ID	Select the appropriate month as the Statement ID.
H	"From" radio button	Click the "From" radio button.
I	From and To boxes	Select the same customer ID in both the From and To boxes.
J	Insert button	Click the Insert button.
K	Print button	Click the Print button and then the Save button when asked if you want to save the changes.
L	OK button (Report Destination window, not shown)	Click the OK button in the Report Destination window to send the report to the default destination, Screen.
M	Print button (Screen Output screen, not shown)	Review the report on the screen, turn your printer on, and click the Print button.
N	OK button (Print window, not shown)	After the Print window opens, click the OK button.

Age Accounts Receivable and
Print Customer Monthly Statements
Dynamics Windows

Receivables Aging Process Window
Sales → *Aging (RO)* **(A)**

Print Receivables Statements Window
Sales → *Statements (RO)* **(F)**

Age Accounts Receivable and
Print Customer Monthly Statements
Detailed Instructions

A. Click *Sales → Aging (RO)*

> *Click Sales → Aging (RO) to open the Receivables Aging Process window.*

B. Review the Aging Date and Change if Necessary

> The default aging date is the current date. Accounts receivable are usually aged as of the end of a period, such as a month, quarter, or year-end.

> *Review the aging date and change if necessary. See step C if you receive a message about the length of time between the aging date and the user date. If you do not receive this message, skip to step D.*

C. If You Receive a Message About Time Between Aging Date and User Date, Click the Continue Button

> *If you receive a message about the length of time between the aging date and the user date click the Continue button.*

D. Click the Process Button

> After the aging date is entered, you can begin the receivables aging process. After the aging process is done, outstanding accounts receivable are sorted into aging categories. Examples include current, 1-30 days, 31-60 days, etc.

> *Click the Process button to perform the accounts receivable aging process.*

E. Click the Cancel Button in the Report Destination Window

> After the aging process is complete, *Microsoft Dynamics GP* prepares an aging report. The aging report will not be used in this project.

> *After the Report Destination window appears, click the Cancel button to cancel printing the aging report.*

> After the outstanding accounts receivable are properly categorized, the next step is to print a customer monthly statement.

F. Click *Sales → Statements (RO)*

➤ *Click Sales → Statements (RO) to open the Print Receivables Statements window.*

G. Select the Appropriate Month as the Statement ID

Microsoft Dynamics GP allows you to set up and save a customized customer monthly statement. For this project, a sample December monthly statement has already been created.

➤ *Use the Statement ID lookup button to select DECEMBER, the customized December customer statement.*

H. Click the "From" Radio Button

The From and To buttons set the range of customer statements to be printed. The statement's default setting is to print all customer statements. To print only one customer's monthly statement, you must first click the From radio button.

➤ *Click the From radio button.*

I. Select the Same Customer ID in both the From and To Boxes

Because you are selecting only one customer's monthly statement, you must enter the chosen customer's Customer ID in both the From and To boxes.

➤ *Use the adjacent lookup buttons to select the chosen customer's Customer ID in both the From and To boxes.*

J. Click the Insert Button

➤ *Click the Insert button in the bottom left corner to insert the customer ID range into the Restrictions box.*

K. Click the Print Button and then the Save Button when Asked if You Want to Save the Changes

 Click the Print button.

Next, the software asks if you want to save the changes to the statement option.

 Click Save when asked if you want to save the changes.

L. Click the OK Button in the Report Destination Window to Send the Report to the Default Destination, Screen

 Click the OK button in the Report Destination window to print the statement to the screen for your review.

M. Review the Report on the Screen, Turn your Printer On, and Click the Print Button

After reviewing the statement on the screen, you can print a hard copy of the statement.

 Turn your printer on. When the printer is ready, click the Print button in the top left corner of the Screen Output window for the customer statement.

N. After the Print Window Opens, Click the OK Button

The next window that appears is the Print window for your printer.

 After the Print window opens, click the OK button to print the statement.

This page is intentionally blank.

Generate Standard Reports

Overview

The *Microsoft Dynamics GP* program contains standard reports for both on-screen review and printing. Standard reports are available in the following areas: Financial, Sales, Purchasing, Inventory, Payroll, and Fixed Assets. This section provides instructions for both viewing standard reports on the screen and printing standard reports.

In addition to the standard reports included with the program, users can customize reports to meet the unique needs of each company. Customized reports are covered in the next section on pages 170-174.

All standard reports are generated through Report windows, an example of which is shown at the top of page 165. The Select Reports section of the Reference Summary Card provides instructions for opening the correct Report window for all standard reports used in this project. After the correct Report window is opened, you can view and print the report by following steps B through I in the Quick Reference Table below.

Quick Reference Table

Step	Box or Other Location	Procedure
A	Reference Summary Card	Follow the instructions on the Reference Summary Card to select the desired report.
B	Options	Click the report option name in the Options box.
C	Insert button	Click the Insert button to move the option to the Print List side.
D	Print button	Click the Print button.
E	Destination check boxes (Report Destination window, bottom of page 165)	Send the report to the Screen by ensuring that the Screen check box is selected and the Printer and File check boxes are not.
F	OK button (Report Destination window)	Click the OK button to view the report on the screen before printing.
G	Screen Output window (page 166)	Review the report on the screen for completeness and accuracy.
H	Print button (Screen Output window, top of page 166)	If printing the report to a printer, click the Print button.
I	OK button (Print window for your printer, not shown)	When the Print window opens, click the OK button.

Generate Standard Reports
Great Plains Windows

Sample Report Window for a Standard Report
(See the last column in the Select Reports section of the Reference Summary Card for instructions to open the correct Report window for each standard report.)

Receivables Trial Balance Reports

File   Edit   Tools   Help   sa Jackson Supply Company 2/1/2010

Clear   Print

Reports:
Aged Trial Balance

Options: Print List:
Aged TB   **B**   **C** Insert >>

Remove

New   Modify

Sample Report Destination Window

Report Destination

Report Information
Name: Aged Trial Balance
Option: T/B
☑ Ask Each Time

Destination
☑ Screen
☐ Printer
☐ File
File Name:
File Format:
⦿ Append   ○ Replace

F OK   Cancel

Generate Standard Reports
Great Plains Windows, continued

Sample Screen Output Window Ⓖ

Screen Output - RM Quick Summary Aged Trial Balance

| File Ⓗ | Tools | Find | Help | | sa Jackson Supply Company 2/1/2010 |

Print | Send To | Modify | 100% | Completed 2 Pages | Page 1

System: 1/26/2008 8:27:56 PM		
User Date: 2/1/2010		

AGED TRIAL BALANCE - SUMMARY
Jackson Supply Company
Receivables Management

Ranges:
					Sorted:
Customer ID:	First - Last		Customer Name:	First - Last	
Salesperson ID:	First - Last		User-Defined 1:	First - Last	
Class ID:	First - Last		Sales Territory:	First - Last	
Document Date:	First - Last				

Customer: 1000CASHCUST **Name:** **Account Type:** Open Item **Aged As**

User-Defined 1:		Salesperson:					
Contact:		Territory:			Current	Past 1-30	Past 31-60
Phone:	( ) - Ext.	Terms:	Cash				
Credit:	Unlimited			**Totals:**	$0.00	$0.00	$0.00

Customer: AIRP0001 **Name:** Airport Inn **Account Type:** Open Item **Aged As**

User-Defined 1:		Salesperson:					
Contact:	James Lilley	Territory:			Current	Past 1-30	Past 31-60
Phone:	(814) 896-1000 Ext. 0000	Terms:	2% 10/Net 30				
Credit:	$15,000.00			**Totals:**	$0.00	$0.00	$0.00

Customer: AMER0001 **Name:** Ameristay International **Account Type:** Open Item **Aged As**

User-Defined 1:		Salesperson:					
Contact:	Manager - Alison Green	Territory:			Current	Past 1-30	Past 31-60
Phone:	(814) 894-4600 Ext. 0000	Terms:	2% 10/Net 30				
Credit:	$15,000.00			**Totals:**	$0.00	$0.00	$0.00

Customer: ANSO0001 **Name:** Anson Lodge **Account Type:** Open Item **Aged As**

User-Defined 1:		Salesperson:					
Contact:	Manager: Steven Ulberg	Territory:			Current	Past 1-30	Past 31-60
Phone:	(814) 894-5000 Ext. 0000	Terms:	2% 10/Net 30				
Credit:	$10,000.00			**Totals:**	$0.00	$0.00	$0.00

Customer: BEST0001 **Name:** Bestway Motor Lodge **Account Type:** Open Item **Aged As**

User-Defined 1:		Salesperson:					
Contact:	Margery Smalley	Territory:			Current	Past 1-30	Past 31-60
Phone:	(814) 895-4000 Ext. 0000	Terms:	2% 10/Net 30				

Generate Standard Reports
Detailed Instructions

A. Follow the Instructions on the Reference Summary Card to Select the Desired Report

The last column in the Select Reports section of the Reference Summary Card provides instructions for opening the correct Report window and selecting the desired report in the Reports box. Note that for the financial statements listed in the table (the first two table entries), you must first change the current date in *Microsoft Dynamics GP* to match the date of the financial statements you are preparing. This step is not required for any of the other reports listed in the table.

Follow the instructions in the last column of the Select Reports section of the Reference Summary Card for the desired report. For example, to select the general ledger trial balance, click Financial → Trial Balance (RE), then use the Reports lookup button to select Quick Summary.

B. Click the Report Option Name in the Options Box

After the report is selected in step A, a list of report options appears in the Options box. For all reports used in this project, there is only one report option.

Click the report option name in the Options box to highlight it.

C. Click the Insert Button to Move the Option to the Print List Side

After the report option is highlighted in the previous step, you must insert the report option into the Print List box. A report cannot be printed to either the screen or to the printer without first being listed in the Print List box.

After the report option is highlighted in the previous step, click the Insert button to insert the report option into the Print List box.

If you insert a report option and later want to remove it from the Print List box, click the report option name in the Print List box and then click the Remove button. An alternative is to close the Report window and start over.

D. Click the Print Button

➤ *Click the Print button to open the Report Destination window.*

E. Send the Report to the Screen by Ensuring that the Screen Check Box is Selected and the Printer and File Check Boxes are not

It is helpful to view a report on the screen before printing a hard copy because errors can be detected before the report is printed.

➤ *Ensure that the Screen check box is selected and the Printer and File check boxes are not.*

F. Click the OK Button to View the Report on the Screen Before Printing

➤ *Click the OK button to view a copy of the selected report on your screen.*

G. Review the Report on the Screen for Completeness and Accuracy

You can review the report on the screen using the Screen Output window, an example of which is shown on page 166. Notice on page 166 that not all of the sample report shown fits on the screen. Sections of a report that are hidden can be viewed using the up, down, left, and right scrolling arrows. Sometimes the font size used on the screen may make the report difficult to read.

➤ *Review the Screen Output window for the selected report, using the available scrolling arrows.*

➤ *If you do not want to print a hard copy of the report on the screen, close the Screen Output window and the Report window. Do not complete steps H and I.*

➤ *If you want to print a hard copy of the report, go to step H if the report on the screen is correct. If there are errors, close the Screen Output window, return to the main Report window, make the necessary changes, and print the revised report to the screen before moving to step H.*

H. If Printing the Report to a Printer, Click the Print Button

➤ *To print a hard copy of the selected report, click the Print button to open the Print window for your computer. If you do not need to print a hard copy, close the Screen Output window and skip the next step.*

I.   When the Print Window Opens, Click the OK Button

The Print window is used to verify information for your printer and to instruct the software to print a hard copy of the selected report.

➤ *Review the contents of the Print window and change if necessary. Click the OK button to print a hard copy of the report.*

Generate Customized Reports for Waren

Overview

The reports discussed on pages 164-169 represent standard reports included in the *Microsoft Dynamics GP* program. Because the standard reports are unlikely to meet the needs of all companies, the software allows users to create customized reports.

For this project, the following customized reports were created for the company used in Chapter 7, Waren Sports Supply: Sales Listing, Cash Receipts Listing, Purchases Listing, Check Listing, and Payroll Listing. This section provides instructions for printing each of the customized reports using the Custom Reports window.

Quick Reference Table

Step	Box or Other Location	Procedure
A	Menu bar	Click *Reports* (from the menu bar) → *Customized* to open the Custom Reports window.
B	Product	Select *Microsoft Dynamics GP* in the Product box.
C	Series*	Select the series for the customized report.*
D	Custom Reports	Click the name of the report you want to print.
E	Insert button	Click the Insert button to insert the selected report name into the Print List box.
F	Print List	Click the selected report name in the Print List box.
G	Destination button	Click the Destination button.
H	Report Destination window (not shown)	Select Screen as the report destination by removing the check mark next to Printer and inserting a check mark next to Screen.
I	Report Destination window (not shown)	Click the OK button.
J	Print button (Custom Reports window)	Click the Print button.
K	Screen Output window (not shown)	Review the report on the screen for completeness and accuracy.
L	Print button (Screen Output window, not shown)	Click the Print button.
M	OK button (Print window for your printer, not shown)	When the Print window opens, click the OK button.

* For the Sales Listing and the Cash Receipts Listing, select "Sales"; for the Purchases Listing and the Check Listing, select "Purchasing"; for the Payroll Listing, select "Payroll."

Generate Customized Reports for Waren
Great Plains Windows

Custom Reports Window
Reports (from the menu bar) → *Customized* Ⓐ

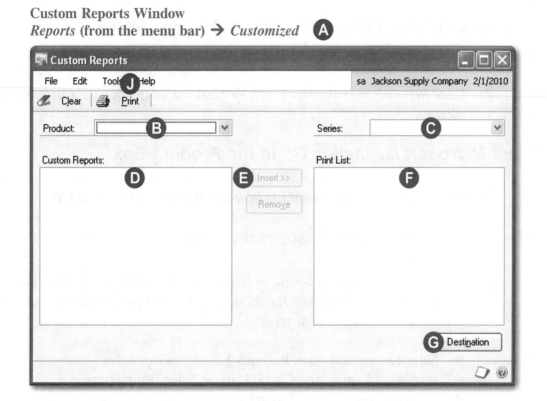

Generate Customized Reports for Waren
Detailed Instructions

A. Click *Reports (from the menu bar)* → *Customized* to Open the Custom Reports Window

➤ *Click Reports (from the menu bar) → Customized to open the Custom Reports window.*

B. Select *Microsoft Dynamics GP* in the Product Box

➤ *Use the Product drop-down list to select Microsoft Dynamics GP.*

C. Select the Series for the Customized Report

➤ *Use the Series drop-down list to select the correct Series for the customized report you are printing.* Use the following information to determine the proper Series for each customized report:

- Sales Listing and Cash Receipts Listing: Select Sales.
- Purchases Listing and Check Listing: Select Purchasing.
- Payroll Listing: Select Payroll.

D. Click the Name of the Report you Want to Print

After selecting the Series in step C, a list of all customized reports for the selected Series appears in the Custom Reports box.

➤ *Click once on the name of the report you want to print.*

E. Click the Insert Button to Insert the Selected Report Name into the Print List Box

➤ *Click the Insert button to insert the selected report name into the Print List box.*

F. Click the Selected Report Name in the Print List Box

➤ *Click once on the selected report name in the Print List box.*

G. Click the Destination Button

All customized reports in *Microsoft Dynamics GP* have the printer as a default print destination. Because it is helpful to review reports before printing a hard copy, you should change the print destination to the screen using the Report Destination window.

➤ *Click the Destination button to open the Report Destination window. This window is the same Report Destination window used for standard reports and is not illustrated in this section. For an illustration of a typical Report Destination window, see page 165.*

H. Select Screen as the Report Destination by Removing the Check Mark Next to Printer and Inserting a Check mark Next to Screen

➤ *Remove the check mark next to the word "Printer" and insert a check mark next to the word "Screen" in the Destination portion of the window.*

I. Click the OK Button

➤ *Click the OK button to accept the screen as the print destination.*

J. Click the Print Button

After clicking the OK button in the previous step, *Microsoft Dynamics GP* returns to the Custom Reports window.

➤ *Click the Print button in the Custom Reports window to print the selected report to the screen.*

K. Review the Report on the Screen for Completeness and Accuracy

The Screen Output window for customized reports is the same as for standard reports and is not illustrated in this section. For an illustration of a typical Screen Output window, see page 166.

➤ *Review the Screen Output window for the selected report, using the available scrolling arrows. If there are errors, close the Screen Output window, return to the Custom Reports window, make the necessary changes, and print the revised report to the screen again.*

L. Click the Print Button

➤ *To print a hard copy of the selected report, click the Print button to open the Print window for your computer.*

M. When the Print Window Opens, Click the OK Button

The Print window is used to verify information for your printer and to instruct *Microsoft Dynamics GP* to print a hard copy of the selected report.

➤ *Review the contents of the Print window and change if necessary. Click the OK button to print a hard copy of the report.*

This page is intentionally blank.

Perform Year-end Closing Procedures

Overview

After all transactions and year-end adjusting entries are posted in *Microsoft Dynamics GP* and all reports are printed, the next step is to close the general ledger for the current year. The year-end closing process in *Microsoft Dynamics GP* closes all income statement accounts to the retained earnings account and sets up the new fiscal year for the company.

Quick Reference Table

Step	Box or Other Location	Procedure
A	*Microsoft Dynamics GP* menu	Click *Tools* → *Setup* → *Company* → *Fiscal Periods*.
B	Year (Fiscal Periods Setup window, top of page 177)	Type the four digits of the new fiscal year.
C	Calculate button	Click the Calculate button; when calculations are done, close the window.
D	Navigation Pane buttons	Click *Financial* → *Year-End Closing (RO)*. Note: this is in the Financial Section of Routines.
E	Close Year button (Year-End Closing window, bottom of page 177)	Click the Close Year button.
F	Year-End Closing Journal (not shown)	Review the Year-End Closing Journal for completeness and accuracy.

Perform Year-end Closing Procedures
Great Plains Windows

Fiscal Periods Setup Window
Tools → Setup → Company → Fiscal Periods **Ⓐ**

Year-End Closing Window
Financial → Year-End Closing (RO) **Ⓓ**

Perform Year-end Closing Procedures
Detailed Instructions

A. Click *Tools (Microsoft Dynamics GP menu)* → *Setup* → *Company* → *Fiscal Periods*

Before the general ledger can be closed for a fiscal year in *Microsoft Dynamics GP*, you must first set up the next fiscal year.

 Click Tools (Microsoft Dynamics GP menu) → *Setup* → *Company* → *Fiscal Periods to open the Fiscal Periods Setup window.*

B. Type the Four Digits of the New Fiscal Year

When you open the Fiscal Periods window, the current year appears in the Year box in the upper left corner. You must type the four digits of the new fiscal year in the box. For example, if you are closing the year ended 12/31/09, type [2010].

 Type the four digits of the new fiscal year.

C. Click the Calculate Button; When Calculations are Done, Close the Window

 Click the Calculate button.

After you click the Calculate button, notice that *Microsoft Dynamics GP* calculates the twelve periods of the next fiscal year. The twelve periods are shown in the scrolling window below.

When the new fiscal period's calculations are done (each month's starting date is correct), close the window.

D. Click *Financial* → *Year-End Closing (RO)*

The final part of *Microsoft Dynamics GP's* year-end closing procedures is to close the general ledger for the current fiscal year.

Click Financial → *Year-End Closing (RO) to open the Year-End Closing window.* Note: this is in the Financial section of Routines.

E. Click the Close Year Button

 Click the Close Year button to complete the year-end closing process for the general ledger for the current fiscal year. Depending on the speed of your computer, this process may take several seconds. A progress window is provided.

F. Review the Year-End Closing Journal for Completeness and Accuracy

After the year-end closing process is complete for the general ledger, *Microsoft Dynamics GP* creates a report that you can view on the screen. This report shows the journal entry that was posted to close all revenue and expense accounts to retained earnings at year-end.

 When the Report Destination window appears, print the report to the screen for your review.

 Close the report after your review.

 Close the Year-End Closing window.

This page is intentionally blank.

APPENDICES

Appendices:

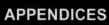
This page is intentionally blank.

Appendix A

Error Correction

Overview

After a transaction is posted in *Microsoft Dynamics GP*, it cannot be edited or deleted. The reason that the software prohibits simply eliminating a posted transaction is to improve internal controls.

Error correction falls into two categories:

1. Void the original transaction and then record the original transaction correctly.
2. Record a transaction to reverse the effect of the original transaction and then record the original transaction correctly.

The first category is inconvenient, but not difficult. The second is more complex and often causes inexperienced users of *Microsoft Dynamics GP* considerable difficulty.

You will most likely use error correction only in Chapters 7 through 9. An option that you may find easier, especially for category 2 errors, is to start the chapter over by reinstalling the *Microsoft Dynamics GP* software. An even better option is to avoid posting transactions that are in error.

The appendix is designed to help you correct errors for the following posted transactions:

CATEGORY 1 (void the original transaction and then record the original transaction correctly)		CATEGORY 2 (record a transaction to reverse the effect of the original transaction and then record the original transaction correctly)	
Transaction or Other Activity	**Appendix Page #**	**Transaction or Other Activity**	**Appendix Page #**
Collect an outstanding account receivable	A-9	Make a credit sale	A-2
Write-off an uncollectible account receivable	A-10	Make a cash sale	A-4
Receive a miscellaneous cash receipt	A-11	Receive goods on a sales return	A-6
Prepare a purchase order	A-13	Receive goods from a purchase order	A-14
Pay a vendor's outstanding invoice	A-17	Prepare a general journal entry	A-22
Purchase goods or services without a purchase order	A-18	Adjust perpetual inventory records	A-23
Pay employees	A-20		

Error Correction — Make a Credit Sale

Overview

After a credit sale invoice is posted through the Invoice Entry window, you cannot edit or delete the invoice. Error correction for credit sales is somewhat complex because of accounts receivable and inventory perpetual records, and because of sales discounts. There are three steps:

(1) Eliminate the incorrectly recorded invoice by recording a sales return.
(2) Apply the sales return transaction to the incorrectly recorded invoice.
(3) Record the original invoice correctly.

(1) Eliminate the Incorrectly Recorded Invoice by Recording a Sales Return

Follow steps A-Q in the quick reference table on page 22 to record a sales return with the following modifications:

- *In the Document No. box, type [REMOVE] and the invoice number you are eliminating. For example, to correct invoice #4536, type [REMOVE4536].*
- *Enter the date of the incorrectly recorded invoice in the Date box. Leave the PO Number box blank.*
- *Enter the same items and quantities that were entered on the incorrectly recorded invoice.*
- *The inventory items should be returned to "On Hand" status.*
- *When reviewing the general ledger account distributions, the accounts and amounts in the correcting transaction must <u>exactly</u> match those from the incorrectly recorded invoice. Therefore, you will have to change certain accounts and/or amounts.* Hint: While recording the correcting entry, use the Inquiry function to determine the posting accounts and amounts from the incorrect invoice. You can do this even while you are using the Invoice Entry window for the correcting transaction.

(2) Apply the Sales Return Transaction to the Incorrectly Recorded Invoice

Follow steps R-Y in the quick reference table on page 22 to apply the correcting sales return transaction to the incorrectly recorded invoice with the following modifications:

- *Use the Document No. lookup button to select the correcting sales return entry.*
- *Enter the date of the incorrectly recorded invoice as the posting date.*
- *Because Microsoft Dynamics GP does not reduce the amount of the discount available, you must change information in two boxes on the screen for the incorrectly recorded invoice.*

  (1) Click the Show button.
  (2) Delete the amount in the Terms Taken box for the incorrect invoice. The amount should be zero.
  (3) Delete the amount in the Apply Amount box for the incorrect invoice and type the total invoice amount from the incorrect invoice. The amount should be the same as the amount in the Original Amount box in the top right portion of the window.

(3) Record the Original Invoice Correctly

Refer to pages 6-12 to record the credit sale invoice correctly. For the invoice number, use the original invoice number but type an "A" at the end of the number. This will permit you to record the remaining invoices in the project without the invoice numbers being out of sequence.

Error Correction — Make a Cash Sale

Overview

After a cash sale invoice is posted through the Invoice Entry window, you cannot edit or delete the invoice. Error correction for cash sales is similar to error correction for credit sales, but there are only two steps:

(1) Eliminate the incorrectly recorded cash sale invoice by recording a sales return.
(2) Record the original cash sale invoice correctly.

(1) Eliminate the Incorrectly Recorded Cash Sale Invoice by Recording a Sales Return

Follow steps A-Q in the quick reference table on page 22 to record a sales return with the following modifications (do not complete steps R-Y for applying the sales return):

- *In the Document No. box, type [REMOVE] and the cash sale invoice number you are eliminating.* For example, to correct cash sale invoice #C-893, type [REMOVE C-893].
- *Enter the date of the incorrectly recorded cash sale invoice in the Date box.*
- *Leave the PO Number box blank.*
- *Enter the same items and quantities that were entered on the incorrectly recorded cash sale invoice.*
- *The inventory items should be returned to "On Hand" status.*
- *Because payment was received on the date of the sale, you must reverse out the effects of the cash receipt portion of the transaction using the Amount Received box.* Do the following:

  (1) *Type the invoice total amount in the Amount Received box.* The Invoice Payment Entry window will open.
  (2) *Click the Insert button in the Invoice Payment Entry window.* Note: the Payment Type default entry, "Cash" is correct as is. Do not change it.

- *When reviewing the general ledger account distributions, the accounts and amounts in the correcting transaction must <u>exactly</u> match those from the incorrectly recorded cash sale invoice. Therefore, you will have to change certain accounts and/or amounts (such as changing the sales returns account to the sales revenue account).* Hint: While recording the correcting entry, use the Inquiry function to determine the posting accounts and amounts from the incorrect invoice. You can do this even while you are using the Invoice Entry window.

(2) Record the Original Cash Sale Invoice Correctly

Refer to pages 14-21 to record the cash sale invoice correctly. For the invoice number, use the original cash sale invoice number but type an "A" at the end of the number. This will permit you to record the remaining cash sale invoices in the project without the document numbers being out of sequence.

Error Correction — Receive Goods on a Sales Return

Overview

After a sales return is posted through the Invoice Entry window and applied to an outstanding invoice, you cannot edit or delete the transaction. Error correction for sales returns is similar to error correction for credit sale invoices, but is somewhat more complex because of applying sales returns to outstanding invoices. There are four steps:

(1) "Unapply" the incorrectly recorded sales return from the customer's original invoice.

(2) Eliminate the incorrectly recorded sales return by recording a correcting invoice transaction.

(3) Apply the incorrectly recorded sales return to the correcting invoice transaction prepared in step (2).

(4) Record and apply the original sales return correctly.

(1) "Unapply" the Incorrectly Recorded Sales Return from the Customer's Original Invoice

Recall that each sales return transaction must be applied to an outstanding customer invoice. The incorrectly recorded sales return was already applied to a customer's outstanding invoice even though it contained an error. Because the sales return has been corrected, you need to "unapply" the incorrect sales return from the customer's invoice before the corrected sales return can be applied.

Follow steps R-Y in the quick reference table on page 22 to unapply the incorrectly recorded sales return from the customer's original invoice. The instructions should be modified as follows:

- *Use the Document No. lookup button to select the incorrectly recorded sales return transaction.*

- *Enter the date of the incorrectly recorded sales return as the posting date.*

- *Instead of inserting a check mark in the check box next to the original invoice, you should remove the check mark to "Unapply" the incorrectly recorded sales return.*

(2) Eliminate the Incorrectly Recorded Sales Return by Recording a Correcting Invoice Transaction

⇒ *Refer to pages 6-12 to record an invoice with the following modifications:*

- *In the Document No. box, type* [REMOVE] *and the sales return document number you are eliminating.* For example, to remove the effects of sales return #5200, type [REMOVE5200].

- *Enter the date of the incorrectly recorded sales return in the Date box. Leave the PO Number box blank.*

- *Enter the same items and quantities that were entered on the incorrectly recorded sales return.*

- *When reviewing the general ledger account distributions, the accounts and amounts in the correcting transaction must <u>exactly</u> match those from the incorrectly recorded sales return. Therefore, you will have to change certain accounts and/or amounts (such as changing the sales revenue account to the sales returns account). The inventory and cost of goods sold do not show in this window. Do not be concerned because they will post automatically after you finish this window and post the transaction.* Hint: While recording the correcting entry, use the Inquiry function to determine the posting accounts and amounts from the incorrect sales return transaction. You can do this even while you are using the Invoice Entry window for the correcting transaction.

(3) Apply the Incorrectly Recorded Sales Return to the Correcting Invoice Transaction Prepared in Step (2)

In order to keep the correcting invoice transaction prepared in step (2) from showing as an outstanding customer invoice in *Microsoft Dynamics GP*, you need to apply the incorrectly recorded sales return transaction to it. The two transactions will cancel each other out, but a transaction trail remains.

⇒ *Follow steps R-Y in the quick reference table on page 22 to apply the incorrectly recorded sales return to the correcting invoice transaction prepared in step (2). The instructions should be modified as follows:*

- *Use the Document No. lookup button to select the incorrectly recorded sales return.*

- *Enter the date of the incorrectly recorded sales return as the posting date.*

- *Apply the incorrectly recorded sales return to the correcting invoice transaction.*

- *Because Microsoft Dynamics GP does not reduce the amount of the discount available, you must change information in two boxes on the screen for the correcting invoice transaction (the "REMOVE" transaction).*

  (1) *Click the Show button and delete the amount in the Terms Taken box for the "REMOVE" transaction. The amount should be zero.*
  (2) *Delete the amount in the Apply Amount box for the "REMOVE" transaction and type the total sales return amount in the Apply Amount box. The amount should be the same as the amount in the Original Amount box in the top right portion of the window.*

(4) Record and Apply the Original Sales Return Correctly

Refer to pages 22-28 to record the sales return correctly and apply the corrected transaction to the customer's original invoice. For the Document No. box, use the original sales return document number but type an A at the end of the number. This will permit you to record the remaining sales returns in the project without the document numbers being out of sequence.

Error Correction — Collect an Outstanding Account Receivable

Overview

After an account receivable collection is posted through the Cash Receipts Entry window, you cannot edit or delete the transaction. Instead, you must complete the following steps:

(1) Void the original account receivable collection using the Receivables Posted Transaction Maintenance window.
(2) Record the original account receivable collection correctly.

(1) Void the Original Account Receivable Collection Using the Receivables Posted Transaction Maintenance Window

 Click Sales → Posted Transactions (T).

 Use the Customer ID lookup button to select the customer whose collection was recorded incorrectly.

 Select Payments in the Document Type box.

 Use the Number lookup button to select the payment number of the collection recorded incorrectly. Hint: When the Open Documents window opens, click the Show button to reveal all detail lines in the scrolling window.

 Review the Posting Date and change it if necessary. The posting date should match the date used in the original transaction.

 Review the window to make sure the proper transaction was selected. If not, reselect the transaction.

 Click the Void button to void the transaction.

(2) Record the Original Account Receivable Collection Correctly

 Refer to the instructions on pages 30-34 to record the account receivable collection correctly, but with the following modification.

When entering the customer's check number, *Microsoft Dynamics GP* will not allow you to enter the same check number used in the transaction that was voided.

 In the Check/Card Number box, type the customer's check number followed by an "A".

Error Correction — Write-off
an Uncollectible Account Receivable

Overview

After an account receivable write-off transaction is posted through the Receivables Transaction Entry window, you cannot edit or delete the transaction. Instead, you must complete the following steps:

(1) Void the original account receivable write-off using the Receivables Posted Transaction Maintenance window.

(2) Record the original account receivable write-off correctly.

(1) Void the Original Account Receivable Write-off Using the Receivables Posted Transaction Maintenance Window

➤ *Click Sales → Posted Transactions (T).*

➤ *Use the Customer ID lookup button to select the customer whose write-off transaction was recorded incorrectly.*

➤ *Select Credit Memo in the Document Type box.*

➤ *Use the Number lookup button to select the credit memo number used for the incorrectly recorded write-off transaction.* Hint: When the Open Documents window opens, click the Show button to reveal the detail lines in the scrolling window.

➤ *Review the Posting Date and change it if necessary. The posting date should match the date used in the original transaction.*

➤ *Review the window to make sure the proper transaction was selected. If not, reselect the transaction.*

➤ *Click the Void button to void the transaction.*

(2) Record the Original Account Receivable Write-off Correctly

➤ *Refer to the instructions on pages 36-41 to record the account receivable write-off correctly.*

Error Correction — Receive a
Miscellaneous Cash Receipt

Overview

After a miscellaneous cash receipt transaction is posted through the Bank Transaction Entry window, you cannot edit or delete the transaction. Instead, you must complete the following three steps:

(1) If a bank deposit was recorded for the miscellaneous cash receipt, void the bank deposit.
(2) Void the original miscellaneous cash receipt transaction using the Bank Transaction Entry window.
(3) Record the original miscellaneous cash receipt transaction correctly.

(1) If a Bank Deposit was Recorded for the Miscellaneous Cash Receipt, Void the Bank Deposit

If a bank deposit was recorded for the miscellaneous cash receipt, you must first void the bank deposit. If there was no bank deposit recorded, skip to step (2).

➤ *Click Financial* ➔ *Bank Deposits (T) to open the Bank Deposit Entry window.*

➤ *Select Void in the Option box.*

➤ *Select the Checkbook ID used in the original bank deposit entry.*

➤ *Use the Deposit Number lookup button to select the deposit for the incorrectly recorded miscellaneous cash receipt transaction.*

➤ *Click the Void button at the top of the window.*

(2) Void the Original Miscellaneous Cash Receipt Transaction Using the Bank Transaction Entry Window

➤ *Click Financial* ➔ *Bank Transactions (T) to open the Bank Transaction Entry window.*

➤ *Select Void Receipt in the Option box.*

➤ *Select the Checkbook ID used for the incorrectly recorded transaction.*

➤ *Use the Number lookup button to select the incorrectly recorded miscellaneous cash receipt transaction.*

➤ *The Transaction Date should match the date of the incorrectly recorded transaction.*

➧ *Type a description in the Description box.* An example description would be: [Void incorrect cash receipt].

➧ *Click the Void button.*

(3) Record the Original Miscellaneous Cash Receipt Transaction Correctly

➧ *Refer to the instructions on pages 42-46 to record the miscellaneous cash receipt transaction correctly.*

Error Correction — Prepare a Purchase Order

Saved purchase orders that have no goods received against them can be edited using the Purchase Order Entry window. To correct a saved purchase order, complete the following steps:

- *If you are not already in the Purchase Order Entry window, click Purchasing → Purchase Order Entry (T).*
- *Use the PO Number lookup button to select the purchase order being corrected. If the desired purchase order is not visible in the scrolling window, click the Redisplay button.*
- *Correct the purchase order information.*
- *Save the revised purchase order.*
- *Close the Purchase Order Entry window.*

Note: Alternatively, you can use the Void button at the top of the window to void the purchase order. After a purchase order is voided, you can then enter a new purchase order with the correct information. After a purchase order is voided, you cannot use the PO number from the original purchase order again. Therefore, it is recommended for this project that you edit the existing purchase order using the instructions above.

Error Correction — Receive Goods from a Purchase Order

Overview

After the receipt of goods from a purchase order is posted through the Receivings Transaction Entry window, you cannot edit or delete the transaction. Instead, you must complete the following steps:

(1) Void the receipt of goods transaction using the Void Open Payables Transactions window.
(2) Adjust the perpetual inventory records to reverse the effects of the incorrectly recorded receipt of goods transaction.
(3) Record the originating purchase order again.
(4) Record the original receipt of goods transaction correctly.

(1) Void the Receipt of Goods Transaction Using the Void Open Payables Transactions Window

Note: If the original Receipt of Goods Transaction that you are voiding here was for only a partial shipment, you will be voiding only the invoice for the goods received. The goods not received yet remain open on the original purchase order. When they are received, they will likely have a different invoice. This receipt and invoice will be processed normally through the Receivings Transaction Entry Window using pages 60-66 of the Reference book.

➤ *Click Purchasing → Void Open Transactions (T) to open the Void Open Payables Transactions window.*

➤ *Use the Vendor ID lookup button to select the vendor from the incorrectly posted transaction.*

➤ *Locate the line in the scrolling window that contains the invoice number from the incorrectly posted transaction. Click the check box on the far right side of the line in the scrolling window to indicate that you want to void this transaction.*

➤ *Click the Void button at the top of the window.*

➤ *Close the Void Open Payables Transactions window.*

(2) Adjust the Perpetual Inventory Records to Reverse the Effects of the Incorrectly Recorded Receipt of Goods Transaction

When *Microsoft Dynamics GP* voids an incorrectly recorded receipt of goods transaction, the program updates the vendor subsidiary record (and eventually the general ledger when the transaction is later posted to the general ledger), but not the perpetual inventory records. You must record an adjustment to the perpetual inventory records that reverses the effects of the incorrectly recorded transaction.

The first step in adjusting the perpetual inventory records is to turn off posting from the Inventory module to the general ledger. This is necessary to avoid double posting the effects of the voided invoice to the general ledger.

➤ *Using the Microsoft Dynamics GP menu, click Tools → Setup → Posting → Posting to open the Posting Setup window.*

➤ *Select Inventory in the Series box.*

➤ *Select Transaction Entry in the Origin list box.*

➤ *Click the check box next to the words "Post to General Ledger" to remove the check mark.*

➤ *Click the Save button and close the Posting Setup window.*

Because the perpetual records were not updated when the invoice was voided, each item received and billed with the original invoice must be removed from the perpetual inventory records. You must record a decrease adjustment for each type of inventory item that equals the quantity received and billed on the original invoice. For example, if 10 units of item #4502 were received and billed on an invoice that was subsequently voided, the perpetual inventory adjustment for item #4502 would be to decrease the quantity by 10. All inventory items from the voided invoice should be adjusted in one transaction.

➤ *Refer to pages 100-104 a perpetual inventory adjustment to remove the items "received" on the voided invoice from the perpetual records.*

After you correct the perpetual records, you must reactivate general ledger posting from the Inventory module.

➤ *Using the Microsoft Dynamics GP menu, click Tools → Setup → Posting → Posting to open the Posting Setup window.*

➤ *Select Inventory in the Series box.*

➤ *Select Transaction Entry in the Origin list box.*

➤ *Click the check box next to the words "Post to General Ledger" to reinstate the check mark.*

➤ *Click the Save button and close the Posting Setup window.*

(3) Record the Originating Purchase Order Again

Recall that the incorrectly recorded receipt of goods transaction relates to a specific purchase order. After goods are received against a purchase order, the purchase order cannot be voided or changed. You must record the originating purchase order again.

➤ Refer to pages 54-59 to record the originating purchase order with the following modifications:

- *In the PO Number box, type the original purchase order number followed by an "A". The program will not allow you to enter the same purchase order number twice.*
- *If the error from the incorrectly recorded transaction goes all the way back to the originating purchase order, be sure to enter the correct information in the Purchase Entry window.*
- *Enter the date of the original purchase order in the Date box.*

Note: If the Receipt of Goods from a Purchase Order that you are correcting here was for a partial shipment, remember that you only voided that part of the original purchase order that was received and recorded incorrectly. Thus, in recording the originating purchase order again, you will not include the items from the original purchase order that have not yet been received. They remain open on the original purchase order and can be recorded and applied against that purchase order when they are received.

(4) Record the Original Receipt of Goods Transaction Correctly

The final step is to record the receipt of goods transaction correctly.

➤ *Refer to pages 60-66 to record the receipt of goods transaction correctly, with the following modifications.*

- *In the Vendor Doc. No. box, type the vendor's invoice number followed by an "A". The program will not allow you to enter the same vendor invoice number twice.*
- *The Date box should match the date of the original transaction.*

Error Correction — Pay a Vendor's Outstanding Invoice

Overview

After a payment of a vendor's outstanding invoice is posted through the Payables Manual Payment Entry window, you cannot edit or delete the transaction. Instead, you must complete the following steps:

(1) Void the original payment transaction using the Void Historical Payables Transactions window.
(2) Record the original payment transaction correctly.

(1) Void the Original Payment Transaction Using the Void Historical Payables Transactions Window

➤ *Click Purchasing → Void Historical Transactions (T) to open the Void Historical Payables Transactions window.*

➤ *Locate the line in the scrolling window that contains the check number from the incorrectly posted payment. Click the check box on the far right side of the line in the scrolling window to indicate that you want to void this check number.*

➤ *Click the Void button at the top of the window.*

➤ *Close the Void Historical Payables Transactions window.*

(2) Record the Original Payment Transaction Correctly

➤ *Refer to the instructions on pages 68-73 to record the payment transaction correctly.* For the Document (check) number, use the original check number but type an A at the end of the number. This will permit you to record the remaining checks in the project without the check numbers being out of sequence.

Error Correction — Purchase Goods or Services Without a Purchase Order

Overview

After a purchase of goods or services without a purchase order transaction is posted through the Payables Transaction Entry window, you cannot edit or delete the transaction. Instead, you must complete the following steps:

(1) Void the payment portion of the original transaction (if applicable).
(2) Void the purchase portion of the original transaction.
(3) Record the original transaction correctly.

(1) Void the Payment Portion of the Original Transaction (if Applicable)

Recall that the Payables Transaction Entry window can be used to record both a vendor's invoice and the corresponding payment of that invoice on the same day. If the incorrectly recorded transaction had a corresponding payment on the same day, you need to void the payment portion of the transaction first (accounts payable debit and cash credit from the original transaction). To do this, complete the steps below. **If the incorrectly recorded transaction did not have a corresponding payment, skip to the next section (Void the Purchase Portion of the Original Transaction).**

➤ *Click Purchasing → Void Historical Transactions (T) to open the Void Historical Payables Transactions window.*

➤ *Locate the line in the scrolling window that contains the check number from the incorrectly posted transaction. Click the check box on the far right side of the line in the scrolling window to indicate that you want to void this check number.*

➤ *Click the Void button at the top of the window.*

➤ *Close the Void Historical Payables Transactions window.*

(2) Void the Purchase Portion of the Original Transaction

The next step is to void the purchase portion of the transaction (the accounts payable credit and expense/asset debit from the original transaction). Complete the following steps:

➥ *Click Purchasing → Void Open Transactions (T) to open the Void Open Payables Transactions window.*

➥ *Use the Vendor ID lookup button to select the vendor from the incorrectly recorded transaction.*

➥ *Locate the line in the scrolling window that contains the purchase transaction you want to void. Click the check box on the far right side of the line in the scrolling window to indicate that you want to void this purchase transaction.*

➥ *Click the Void button at the top of the window.*

➥ *Close the Void Open Payables Transactions window.*

(3) Record the Original Purchase Transaction Correctly

➥ *Refer to the instructions on pages 74-79 to record the purchase transaction correctly. Modify the instructions as follows:*

- *In the Document Number box, type the vendor's original invoice number, followed by an "A".* The software will not let you enter the same vendor's invoice number even though the previous transaction was voided.
- *In the Payables Check Entry window (for purchases with a corresponding payment only), use the original check number but type an "A" at the end of the number.* This will permit you to record the remaining checks in the project without the check numbers being out of sequence.

Error Correction — Pay Employees

Overview

After a payroll transactions are posted through the windows shown on pages 84 and 85, you cannot edit or delete any of the underlying transactions. Instead, you must complete the following steps:

(1) Void the original payroll checks that are in error using the Void Payroll Checks window.
(2) Create a new Batch ID for the correcting transactions.
(3) Record the original payroll transactions correctly.

(1) Void the Original Payroll Checks Using the Void Payroll Checks Window

You can void payroll checks for a specific pay run using the Void Payroll Checks window.

➤ *Change the user date to the date of the payroll check(s) you are going to void.*

➤ *Click HR & Payroll ➔ Void Checks (T) to open the Void Payroll Checks window.*

➤ *Select the Checkbook ID used for the original payroll checks.*

➤ *Click the Redisplay button in the right middle portion of the window.*

➤ *Locate the lines in the scrolling window that contain the payroll check numbers from the pay run you are voiding. Click the check box next to each check in the pay run.*

➤ *Review to ensure that the Check Date and Posting Date are the same as the date from the original payroll checks.*

➤ *Click the Process button at the bottom of the window.*

➤ *Click the Cancel button when the Print window opens.*

(2) Create a New Batch ID for the Correcting Transactions

You must create a Batch ID for the corrected payroll transactions you will be entering.

→ *Click HR & Payroll → Batches (T) to access the Payroll Batch Entry window.*

→ *Type a name for the batch you are creating in the Batch ID box.* An example for a corrected November 30, 2009 pay run would be "NEW113009."

→ *Select "Computer Checks" in the Origin box.*

→ *Click the Save button and then close the Payroll Batch Entry window.*

(3) Record the Original Payroll Transactions Correctly

→ *Refer to the instructions on pages 82-92 to record the corrected payroll transactions. Modify the instructions as follows:*

(1) For step B, select the Batch ID you created in step (2) for the correcting payroll transactions.

(2) For step V, you can either enter a new starting check number or you can put an "A" in front of the original starting check number from the voided transactions.

Error Correction — Prepare a
General Journal Entry

Overview

After a general journal entry is posted through the Transaction Entry window, it cannot be edited or deleted. To correct an error, complete the following steps:

(1) Record another general journal entry that reverses the effects of the incorrectly recorded journal entry.

(2) Record the general journal entry correctly.

(1) Record Another General Journal Entry that Reverses the Effects of the Incorrectly Recorded Journal Entry

 Refer to the instructions on pages 94-98 to record a general journal entry that reverses the effects of the incorrectly recorded inventory adjustment. For example, if the Cash account was debited for $1,400.00 in the incorrectly recorded journal entry, you need to credit the Cash account for $1,400.00 in this entry.

(2) Record the General Journal Entry Correctly

 Refer to the instructions on pages 94-98 to record the general journal entry correctly.

Error Correction — Adjust Perpetual Inventory Records

Overview

After a transaction is posted to adjust perpetual inventory records through the Item Transaction Entry window, it cannot be edited or deleted. To correct an error, complete the following steps:

(1) Record an adjustment to the perpetual records that reverses the effects of the incorrectly recorded inventory adjustment.

(2) Record the inventory adjustment correctly.

(1) Record an Adjustment to the Perpetual Records that Reverses the Effects of the Incorrectly Recorded Inventory Adjustment

➤ *Refer to the instructions on pages 100-104 to record an adjustment to the perpetual inventory records that reverses the effects of the incorrectly recorded inventory adjustment.* For example, if the quantity adjustment for an inventory item was +8 in the original adjustment transaction, type [-8] in the Quantity box for that item.

(2) Record the Inventory Adjustment Correctly

➤ *Refer to the instructions on pages 100-104 to record the adjustment to the perpetual inventory records correctly.*

This page is intentionally blank.

Appendix B

Excel PivotTable Instructions

Overview

The purpose of an Excel PivotTable report is to permit summarization and a more detailed analysis of data in an Excel spreadsheet. An Excel PivotTable is often set up in a matrix format showing data in columns and rows. They are easy to set up and are useful for many types of data analysis. The following instructions are intended for and sufficient for the problems in this project. These instructions assume that you are using Excel 2003 or higher. If you are using a different version of Excel, the commands and instructions may differ slightly.

(1) To begin you must have data in an Excel file that has been exported from *Microsoft Dynamics GP* through SmartList. Each Excel column must have a title. At least one of the columns must include numerical data such as dollar amounts, inventory quantities, or hours worked. To illustrate the use of an Excel PivotTable, example Excel data is shown below.

Date	Employee	Hours	Department
1/15	Charles	14	A
1/15	Charles	26	B
1/15	James	11	A
1/15	James	8	B
1/15	James	20	C
1/15	Fox	37	B
1/15	Fox	6	C

(2) Next, you must decide how you would like the data organized. In this example assume that you want an analysis of the payroll hours in each department, by employee. You also decide that you want the employee name in the rows and the departments in the columns. You must decide the organization for each PivotTable application.

(3) ➡️ *Click on any* **one nonnumeric cell where there is information you want summarized.** **Note: this is easy to forget.** In this case click on cell D5, but it doesn't matter which cell you click on as long as it is a nonnumeric cell within the table.

(4)   *Click Data → PivotTable List and PivotChart Report*. The following PivotTable and PivotChart Wizard window appears on the screen:

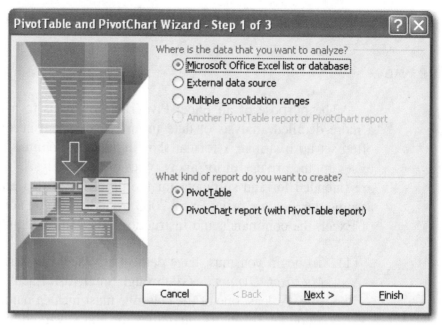

(5)   *Make sure the Microsoft Office Excel list or database and PivotTable radio buttons are marked. Then click Finish.* The following illustration shows how the entire Excel screen should appear after you click the Finish button:

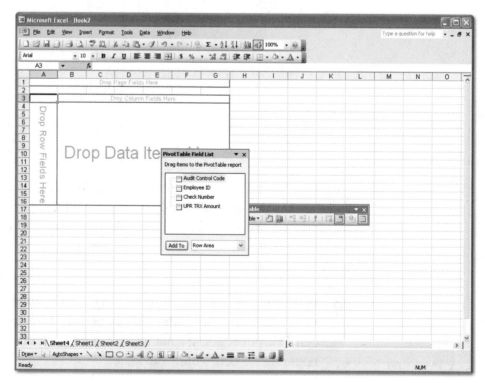

The window on the top left is the PivotTable Report, where the final data will appear when you are finished. The window in the middle is the PivotTable Field List, which is used to set up the PivotTable Report. The additional window is the PivotTable toolbar. Note: you can move the PivotTable Field List window in front of the toolbar by clicking on the PivotTable Field List window.

(6) ➡️ *Click on and drag Employee from the PivotTable Field List to the Drop Row Fields Here on the PivotTable report.* Notice that Employee in the PivotTable Field List now appears in bold type, indicating that it has been used.

(7) ➡️ *Next, click on and drag Department to the Drop Column Field List Here. Then click on and drag Hours to the Drop Data Items Here.* You must use only numeric data in the Drop Data Items Here. The table will appear like the one below. Observe that summarization occurred by combining all hours for each employee and department as well as preparing a matrix with totals. Also note that Date was not used on the PivotTable Field List. This causes no problems.

Sum of Hours	Department ▼			
Employee ▼	A	B	C	Grand Total
Charles	14	26		40
Fox		37	6	43
James	11	8	20	39
Grand Total	25	71	26	122

(8) There are additional features that you will find helpful:

➡️ *Click any cell of the matrix and the PivotTable Field List will disappear.*

➡️ *Click any cell within the matrix and the PivotTable Field List will reappear.*

➡️ *Click and drag on Employee on the Matrix and drag it off the matrix.*

➡️ *Click and drag Date from the PivotTable Field List to the Drop Row Fields.*

➡️ *Click on the drop down arrow next to employee and click on Show All to eliminate all check marks. Now Click on Charles and Fox and click OK.* You can do the same with columns or rows. This feature adds more flexibility to the tool.

➡️ *Change the matrix to appear as it did before step 8.*

You cannot sort or change data in a PivotTable. However, you can copy the table to another Excel worksheet and then make the type of changes available on any Excel worksheet.

(9) ➤ *First, hide the PivotTable Field List and PivotTable toolbar.*

➤ *Next, copy the PivotTable to a new Excel worksheet in the same file. To do so you must first highlight all rows (not just those in the PivotTable report) starting with the names on the PivotTable Report that came from the PivotTable Field List. In this case you will highlight all rows starting with row 4, down to row 8. You will then copy and paste to a new worksheet. It should appear as the one below.* (If you try to copy and paste the entire worksheet, you will get the same PivotTable report.)

You will now have a file with three worksheets: The original Excel file that you downloaded from *Microsoft Dynamics GP*, a PivotTable Report, and an Excel file with the same data as the PivotTable Report. It is useful to rename those worksheets to so you can easily identify each one in the Excel file.

Appendix C

SmartList Guidance

Guidelines for Selecting Folders and Columns

To obtain and analyze information for the assigned problems using SmartList, the following guidance is suggested:

1. Carefully read the problem to fully understand the information needs. Make sure you will be using SmartList to obtain the information before you use this appendix.
2. Decide the cycle you are dealing with and locate it in the next section called "Specific Folder and Column Guidance."
3. Decide the folder within the cycle from the choices listed in the next section. All folders needed to complete the problems are included below each cycle heading. Consider the applicability of the first folder below each cycle heading before considering the next folder down. Guidance is provided for each folder.
4. After deciding and clicking on the folder, decide the columns based on the information needed to complete the problem. Use only one or more of the columns included below each folder heading. You can ignore all other columns in the folder window.

Additional hints to reduce processing and exporting time:

1. The number of transactions or other items in a window can often be greatly reduced by using Search to eliminate zero balances.
2. If more than 1000 transactions or other items are indicated in the count box, there is no time cost to changing it a large number, such as 50,000.
3. If more than 1000 transactions or other items are indicated in the count box, it is usually convenient to finalize all columns and searches before clicking OK to include all items in the window.

Specific Folder and Column Guidance

Revenue Cycle

Customers folder. Use this folder unless data for a period of time is needed.

Column	City
Column	Customer Balance (Balance receivable)
Column	Customer Name
Column	State
Column	Total Costs LYR (Total cost last year)

Column	Total Costs YTD (Total cost year to date)
Column	Total Discounts Taken LYR (Total discounts taken last year)
Column	Total Discounts Taken YTD (Total discounts taken year to date)
Column	Total Sales LYR (Total sales last year)
Column	Total Sales YTD Total sales year to date)

Sales Transactions folder. Use this folder when data for a period of time is needed.

Column	Customer Name
Column	Document Amount
Column	Document Date
Column	SOP Type (Type of sales transaction such as invoice or payment)
Column	State

Expenditures Cycle

Vendors folder. Use this folder unless data for a period of time is needed.

Column	Amount Paid LYR (amount paid last year)
Column	Amount Paid YTD (amount paid year to date)
Column	City
Column	Current Balance
Column	State
Column	Vendor Name

Payables Transactions folder. Use this folder when data for a period of time is needed.

Column	Document Amount (total amount of the transactions)
Column	Document Date
Column	Document Type (Type of transaction such as invoice, purchase order, or payment)
Column	Vendor ID
Column	Vendor Name

Payroll Cycle

Employees folder. Use this folder unless data for a period of time is needed.

Column	Birth Date
Column	Birth Month
Column	Employee ID
Column	First Name
Column	Last Name
Column	State

Payroll Historical Transactions folder. Use this folder when data for a period of time is needed.

Note: Special care is required for obtaining information about gross pay. The UPR TRX Amount column includes gross pay, but also withholdings, as positive numbers. To obtain gross pay, Search must limit The UPR TRX Amount column to Pay Codes by the use of the Payroll Record Type column.

Column	Check Date
Column	City
Column	First Name
Column	Last Name
Column	Payroll Code (such as Salary, Bonus, Commission)
Column	Payroll Record Type [such as Pay Codes (Gross Pay), State Taxes and Benefits]
Column	State
Column	UPR TRX Amount (Gross Payroll and deductions, individually listed)

Inventory

Items folder. Use this folder unless a period of time or inventory quantities on hand are needed.

Column	Current Cost (Unit cost)
Column	Item Description
Column	Item Number
Column	Item Type

Item Quantities folder. Use folder when units on hand are needed.

Column	Current Cost (Unit cost)
Column	Item Description
Column	Item Number
Column	Record Type
Column	QTY on Hand (Quantity on hand)

Payables Transactions folder. Use this folder when data for a period of time is needed.

Column	Current Trx Amount (total amount of the transactions)
Column	Document Date
Column	Document Type (Type of transaction, such as invoice, purchase order, or payment)
Column	Vendor ID
Column	Vendor Name

NOTES:
Use this page to accumulate important notes.

NOTES:
Use this page to accumulate important notes.

NOTES:

Use this page to accumulate important notes.

NOTES:

Use this page to accumulate important notes.

NOTES:

Use this page to accumulate important notes.